Let GOD'S WORD EMPOWER *Your* PRAYERS

STORMIE OMARTIAN

HARVEST HOUSE PUBLISHERS
EUGENE, OREGON

Cover by Left Coast Design, Portland, Oregon

Cover illustration © tang / Shutterstock

Author back cover photo © Michael Gomez Photography

LET GOD'S WORD EMPOWER YOUR PRAYERS
These devotions are taken from *The Power of a Praying® Woman Bible*.
Copyright © 2008 by Stormie Omartian
Published by Harvest House Publishers
Eugene, Oregon 97402
www.harvesthousepublishers.com

ISBN 978-0-7369-6566-8 (pbk.)
ISBN 978-0-7369-6567-5 (eBook)

Printed in the United States of America

15 16 17 18 19 20 21 22 23 24 / VP-JH / 10 9 8 7 6 5 4 3 2 1

Contents

INTRODUCTION

God's Word is living and powerful. People who know God and read His Word often already understand that. But what many of us may not realize is how powerful our prayers can be when we include God's Word *in* them. Whenever we do that, it not only gives us a solid foundation of truth upon which to base our prayers, but it also grows our faith even as we are praying. The reason to include Scripture in our prayers is not to remind God of what He said. He already knows and He does not forget. It is *we* who need to be reminded because we *do* forget. Or we can succumb to doubt. Or perhaps we have not truly understood what the Bible says. Or maybe we have not considered certain verses of Scripture as being applicable to specific subjects about which we want to pray. Whatever the reason, weaving God's truth into our prayers is life-changing.

It is my prayer that after you have read the Scriptures and devotions in this book, and have prayed the prayers that follow, you will be inspired to include Scripture in your own individual prayers as often as you can. Even if you don't specifically quote a verse word for word—although that is very effective—having your prayer *inspired* by God's Word is powerful as well.

As you read and pray through this book, God will surely impress upon your heart to pray about other specific things, or He may give you knowledge, wisdom, and insight that you want to write down. If so, there are pages at the end of the book for that purpose. You will be amazed at how writing down what you hear from God—or want to *say* to God—will bless and strengthen you. Plus, it delights Him to hear from you that you love *Him* and His *Word*. And pleasing God is the best reward of all.

Stormie Omartian

1

The POWER of PRAYING for OTHERS

Colossians 1:9-14

*"For this reason, since the day we heard about you, we
have not stopped praying for you and asking God to
fill you with the knowledge of his will through all
spiritual wisdom and understanding" (Colossians 1:9).*

For all the people we care about—parents, children, a spouse,
friends, family, neighbors, coworkers, or people in need around
the world—one of the best things we can do for them is pray. We
may not be able to provide them with good health, financial security,
or protection from all harm. But we can pray that *God* will heal
them, provide for them, and keep them safe.

The promise to pray for others is one of the finest gifts we can
give. Every time we seek the presence of God and the release of His
power on behalf of someone else, great things happen. It is the most
effective way we can touch others and make a difference in their lives.

The most important thing we can pray about for others is that
they will know God better and that He will help them understand
His will, grow in spiritual wisdom, and live lives that honor Him.
We can pray that they will become more like Him and bear the
fruit of His Spirit.

When we pray for others, we are asking God to make His presence known in their lives. We are asking Him to open their heart so
they can hear from Him. That doesn't mean there will always be an
immediate response. Sometimes it can take days, weeks, months, or
even years. But our prayers are never lost or meaningless. If we are
praying, something is happening in the lives of those for whom we

pray, whether we see it or not. Everything that needs to happen in our lives and in the lives of our loved ones cannot happen without the presence and power of God. Prayer invites and ignites both.

⌒⌒⌒∽⌒⌒⌒

Lord, I pray for the people You have put in my life and on my heart. Fill them with wisdom and understanding and the knowledge of Your will so that they will stay on the path You have for them. I pray they will learn to hear Your voice and come to know You better, so that they can have a closer walk with You. I pray that You will help me to do as Paul did in Your Word and not stop praying for people. Help me to keep praying, even when I don't yet see the answers to my prayers manifesting in their lives. In Jesus' name I pray.

2
PRAYING *on* BEHALF *of* PEOPLE

  Read and Consider
Exodus 8:8-11,28-29; 9:27-30; 10:16-19

*"Pharaoh quickly summoned Moses and Aaron and
said, 'I have sinned against the LORD your God
and against you. Now forgive my sin once more
and pray to the LORD your God to take this deadly
plague away from me'" (Exodus 10:16-17).*

Have you ever tried to share your faith with an unbelieving
friend, coworker, or employer, only to have that person demonstrate disinterest or even downright hostility? Those around you
may reject your concern for them and ignore their own need for a
Savior. However, if a crisis comes, those same people will allow you
to pray for them. They may even seek you out—asking for your
prayers, knowing you have a "hotline" to heaven.

This becomes extremely difficult when we are called to pray
for those who have hurt us. In the Sermon on the Mount, Jesus
instructed His followers to disregard the conventional wisdom of
the time regarding enemies and practice love through intercession
instead. "You have heard that it was said, 'Love your neighbor and
hate your enemy.' But I tell you: Love your enemies and pray for
those who persecute you, that you may be sons of your Father in
heaven" (Matthew 5:43-45).

Pharaoh put all his faith in the ability of his wise men, sorcerers,
and magicians to use their secret arts to perform miracles. But when
the plagues were clearly "the finger of God," Pharaoh turned to
Moses for help, the one man he knew could truly intercede.

The unbelievers in your world should be able to tell by your life that you are a praying person and that they can depend on you to intercede for them with the only One who can truly make a difference.

~ ⁓⁓⁓ ~

God, help me to learn to pray in power. Increase my faith to believe for the answers to my prayers. Enable me to become an intercessor for others—especially those who do not know You. I pray that everyone around me will be able to recognize by my life that I am a person of great faith and power in prayer, and that they can trust in the God to whom I pray. Although Pharaoh—in Your Word—pridefully resisted You and Your messenger, Moses, it was actually Moses whom Pharaoh turned to when he had been humbled. I pray that unbelievers will see so much of Your love in me that they will ask me to pray for them and to tell them more about You. In Jesus' name I pray.

3

FINDING FAITH *to* WAIT
for the ANSWER

"Then he continued, 'Do not be afraid, Daniel.
Since the first day that you set your mind to gain
understanding and to humble yourself before your
God, your words were heard, and I have come in
response to them. But the prince of the Persian kingdom
resisted me twenty-one days'" (Daniel 10:12-13).

Have you ever waited anxiously for a promised letter or package to arrive, only to have days, weeks, or maybe even months pass by with no sign of it? How do you know for certain that it was placed in the mail in the first place or that it wasn't delivered to the wrong address?

When it comes to prayer, most of us will have times when we wonder whether the answer to our request has been "lost." Did God hear us at all, and is He planning to respond?

The book of Daniel contains one of the most encouraging yet sobering conversations recorded in the Bible when it comes to receiving an answer to prayer. Daniel had been faithfully fasting and praying for weeks without seeing any response. After 21 days, he had a vision of an angelic being who appeared to him and told him the reason for the delay: A spiritual battle was being waged in the heavens. Daniel was told that the messenger had been sent in response to his prayers from the first day, but he had been detained by opposition from "the prince of the Persian kingdom," a reference to an evil supernatural force. When Daniel persisted in prayer, help was sent to the first messenger in the form of the archangel Michael, and the messenger finally reached Daniel with a word from God for the future.

What an encouragement this is for us! God has promised to hear our prayers when we come to Him in faith, but we need to remember that Satan may throw obstacles in the way of our receiving the answers God has sent. What are we to do? Continue to pray! The prayers of a righteous man or woman are powerful and effective (James 5:16). Don't give up when the answer doesn't come right away. God hears and will answer. You have His Word on it!

~~~

Heavenly Father, help me to wait patiently for the answers to my prayers. Increase my faith to know that when I pray, You hear the cries of my heart and will answer in Your perfect timing and Your perfect way. Help me to continue to pray and not give up, no matter how long it takes or how many obstacles the enemy throws in my path. Just as Daniel—in Your Word—prayed and the answer to his prayer was set in motion immediately, yet in the weeks it took for the answer to manifest, Daniel did not stop praying. Help me to not stop praying and not give place to discouragement if I don't see answers right away. Help me to trust that You have heard my prayer and will answer in Your way and in Your perfect timing. In Jesus' name I pray.

4

GOD LOOKS *on* YOUR HEART

∞ Read and Consider ∞
1 Samuel 16:1-13

"But the LORD said to Samuel, 'Do not consider
his appearance or his height, for I have rejected
him. The LORD does not look at the things man
looks at. Man looks at the outward appearance, but
the LORD looks at the heart'" (1 Samuel 16:7).

Isn't it comforting to know that God does not judge us in the same way that other people often judge us? Or even in the harsh way in which we sometimes judge ourselves? God is concerned with what is in our hearts. That means He cares about our thoughts, passions, attitudes, and whether we trust in Him and love His ways. He does not place value on our outward looks, social status, financial standing, or any other external measure that the world considers so important.

God's selection of David—someone known as a man after God's own heart—demonstrates God's emphasis on internal rather than external characteristics. David's status in his family was so low that he wasn't even called in to meet with Samuel. He was merely the youngest son, out in the fields tending the sheep. However, David was God's choice to be the king of Israel, to perform great deeds, and to be part of the family line that would produce the Savior whom God would provide for Israel. Clearly, God did not see David in the same way that even his own family saw him.

What is God seeing in your heart today? Take a heart inventory right now. First, pray that God would reveal and then remove anything in your heart that doesn't belong there—resentments, anger, sinful thoughts. Second, pray for big things, knowing that if God can use a young shepherd boy, He can use anyone in a big way! Make your heart available to God's power and see what amazing things He will do through you.

Dear Lord, I am so grateful that You do not judge me the way people do. Thank You that You look on my heart to see my thoughts, attitudes, and love for You. Show me anything in my heart that should not be there, and I will confess it before You. Remove all sinful desires and fill my heart with Your love, peace, and joy. Make me like David—a person after Your own heart. Create in me a clean heart and renew a right Spirit within me. In Jesus' name I pray.

5

GOD HEARS YOU WHEN YOU PRAY

∽ Read and Consider ∽

Psalm 116

"I love the LORD, for he heard my voice; he heard my cry for mercy. Because he turned his ear to me, I will call on him as long as I live" (Psalm 116:1-2).

Do you have someone in your life who listens to you—I mean truly *listens*? Maybe it's a sister or a close friend, or even a coworker who is empathetic. If so, you are blessed. We've all experienced times when it seems as if everyone we know is either too busy or too distracted by their own problems to sit and listen to the cries of our heart. There are few times as lonely as when we are hurting and have no one to tell.

As a child of God, however, you always have someone who will listen to you: God Himself!

Over and over again we find these declarations in the psalms: "God has surely listened and heard my voice in prayer" (66:19). "I waited patiently for the LORD; he turned to me and heard my cry" (40:1). Waiting is never easy, but when the answer to one of your prayers comes, you know without a doubt that God has heard your cries.

God is never so far away that He cannot hear us. Scripture tells us that He turns His ear to us, and it is never a deaf ear. He loves us. He is ever present in our lives. And He hears us when we call to Him.

Never doubt that you have Someone in your life who is always willing to listen. And He alone has the power to change the situation you are facing. Take comfort in the reality that you are loved by God, and He has your best interests at heart. "Be at rest once more, O my soul, for the LORD has been good to you" (116:7).

Lord, I take great comfort in knowing You hear my prayers. Your Word tells me You listen and are never far away so that You cannot hear when I call. Help me to be patient to wait for Your answers, to not lose heart, and to never fear that You have not heard. Help me to trust You enough every day of my life to pray for all that concerns me. Help me to take any feeling of loneliness as a reminder that I need to talk to You. I will call upon You as long as I live because You have said in Your Word that You are always with Me. In Jesus' name I pray.

6

CREATING *a* SYMPHONY *of* PRAYER

Matthew 18:18-20

"Again, I tell you that if two of you on earth agree
about anything you ask for, it will be done for you
by my Father in heaven" (Matthew 18:19).

One of the first things we need to learn about praying with others is the need for unity. Jesus said "If you agree...it will be done." That word *agree* is very important. The Greek word for "unity" is *sumphoneo*. It's where we get the word "symphony." In order to have harmony, there are a number of things we need to agree on.

First of all, we need to agree on the basics, which are the very foundation of our faith. Foremost among these is that Jesus is "the way and the truth and the life" and "no one comes to the Father except through" Him (John 14:6). We must also agree that the Bible is inerrant—without fault in its original translation—and inspired by God. We agree that Jesus was born of a virgin and lived a sinless life, that He died for our sins and rose from the dead, and that whoever believes in Him will have everlasting life.

Second, we need to be in agreement about what we are requesting from God. For example, if your marriage is in trouble, you can pray with your spouse or with a trusted friend and agree together that marriage is a covenant ordained by God. Then ask God to be at the center of your marriage and a reflection of Christ's love for His people (Ephesians 5:31-32). Or another example is if you are in need or struggling in an area, you can join one or more people and agree that Satan will not have victory in this situation.

The Bible says that one can put a thousand to flight and two can put ten thousand to flight (Deuteronomy 32:30). If you do the math, you will see how powerful two or more people can be when they join together and agree in prayer about whatever concerns them.

Unity within the body of Christ is extremely important to God, and unity in prayer is a critical part of that. The very night He was betrayed, Jesus prayed for all believers everywhere that we might experience true unity. "May they be brought to complete unity to let the world know that you sent me and have loved them even as you have loved me" (John 17:23).

When we agree together in prayer, our words create a rich symphony of intercession that is carried to the very throne of God. Nothing is more beautiful to the ear of the Lord than the sound of the unified prayers of His people. Let the music begin.

‹∾∾⊃C⊂∾∾›

Lord, help me to find believers with whom I can agree in prayer on a regular basis. I pray we will be in agreement about the truth of Your Word and the power of Your Holy Spirit. You have said that one can put a thousand to flight and two can put ten thousand to flight. I pray for enough prayer partners to put all of the enemy's forces attacking our lives to flight. You have said in Your Word that if two of us agree about anything we ask for, You will do it for us. Thank You for that precious promise. In Jesus' name I pray.

7

BE BOLD *to* ASK

<del>∽</del> Read and Consider <del>∽</del>
1 Chronicles 4:9-10

*"Jabez cried out to the God of Israel, 'Oh, that you would
bless me and enlarge my territory! Let your hand be with
me, and keep me from harm so that I will be free from
pain.' And God granted his request" (1 Chronicles 4:10).*

Apart from these two verses, Jabez doesn't show up anywhere else
in Scripture. Yet his brief mention here left a lasting impression.
He prayed boldly, and then "God granted his request."

Jabez, whose name sounded like the Hebrew word for "pain,"
made four requests: for God's blessing ("bless me"), for God's provision ("enlarge my territory"), for God's presence ("let your hand be
with me"), and for God's protection ("keep me from harm"). All of
these things are what God wants for us. It is God's pleasure to bless
us and provide for us, to be with us and protect us. But He wants us
to pray and ask. And so often we don't. Too often we think we don't
deserve His blessings or that it is being selfish to ask. Sometimes
we pursue things in our own strength and fail to recognize God's
goodness in wanting to be our provider. Often we don't want to
seem as if we are asking for too much, as if God is limited in what
He has to give.

If you have ever had thoughts like that, consider the words of
Jesus when He said, "Your Father has been pleased to give you the
kingdom" (Luke 12:32). That sounds like He wants to give us more
than we realize.

Have you ever prayed boldly like Jabez did? If not, start by
thanking God for all He has already given you and then ask for

the desires of your heart. Ask Him to bless you so you can serve His purposes and bless others.

Don't worry that in asking boldly you will ask for too much. God is not going to give you something that is not good for you or before you are ready to receive it. He will always answer your prayers according to His will and in His perfect timing.

God, I thank You for all You have given me. I pray for Your continued blessings, provision, and protection. I pray Your presence will always be with me wherever I go and no matter what happens. Thank You that You are pleased to share Yourself and Your kingdom with me. Enable me to give back to You by helping and blessing others. Teach me how to pray according to Your will. Thank You that You will always be my Protector and Provider. Thank You for all of Your blessings on my life. In Jesus' name I pray.

8

HAVING PEACE ABOUT YOUR FUTURE

⌒⌒ Read and Consider ⌒⌒

Isaiah 26:1-9

"You will keep in perfect peace him whose mind is steadfast, because he trusts in you" (Isaiah 26:3).

We all would like to experience "perfect peace," but as we look around at our world, at our lives, at our futures, it's hard to imagine that the peace we experience can ever be perfect. Although God promises us a future full of hope and blessing, it doesn't just happen automatically. There are some things *we* have to do. One of them is to pray (Jeremiah 29:11-13). Another is to obey God.

Every time you pray and obey, you are investing in your future. Although you live in a world where everything in your life can change in an instant, and you can't be certain what tomorrow will bring, God is unchanging. Although you may not know the specific details about what is ahead, you can trust that God knows. And He will get you safely where you need to go. In fact, the way to get to the future God has for you is to walk closely with Him today.

Walking with God doesn't mean there won't be obstacles. Satan will see to it that there are. While God has a plan for your future that is good, the devil has one too, and it's not good. But the devil's plan for your life cannot succeed as long as you are walking with God, living in obedience to His ways, worshipping only Him, standing strong in His Word, and praying without ceasing.

Your future is in *God's* hands. The only thing that is important is what *He* says about it. He doesn't want you to be concerned

23

about your future anyway. He wants you to be concerned with *Him,* because *He* is your future. Remember that you are God's child, and He loves you. As you *walk* with Him, you will become more like Him every day (1 John 3:1-3). As you *look* to Him, you will be "transformed into his likeness with ever-increasing glory, which comes from the Lord, who is the Spirit" (2 Corinthians 3:18). As you *live* with Him, He will take you from strength to strength.

God is looking for people who will be committed to living His way and stepping into the purposes He has for their lives. You are one of those people. I pray that you will be equipped and ready when God says, "Now is the time," and the doors of opportunity open. Just keep doing what's right, and when you least expect it, you will get a call from God giving you your assignment.

Perfect peace can be a reality. Remember, God "is able to do immeasurably more than all we ask or imagine, according to his power that is at work within us" (Ephesians 3:20). He has more for you than you can imagine. And now may "the God of hope fill you with all joy and peace as you trust in him, so that you may overflow with hope by the power of the Holy Spirit" (Romans 15:13). Stay focused on God. As Isaiah wrote, God will keep you in "perfect peace" because you trust in Him.

⁂

Dear God, the only reason I have peace about the future
is because my future is found in You. Even though I
don't know the details about what is to come, I know
You know everything, and my future is in Your hands.
Help me to walk faithfully with You every day—in
prayer and in Your Word—so that I can move into
the purposes You have for my life. Help me to keep
my mind focused on You and Your truth at all times
so that I will live in the peace You have for me.
In Jesus' name I pray.

9

WHEN WE HAVE *to* WAIT

∽ Read and Consider ∽

Genesis 15:1-6

*"After this, the word of the LORD came to Abram in a vision:
'Do not be afraid, Abram. I am your shield, your very great
reward.' But Abram said, 'O Sovereign LORD, what can
you give me since I remain childless and the one who will
inherit my estate is Eliezer of Damascus?'" (Genesis 15:1-2).*

Can't you just hear the exasperation in Abram's voice? "God, I appreciate that You're my shield and reward. That's great and all. Don't think I don't appreciate it, but...what I *really* want is for You to fulfill Your promise of descendants. Let's get on with that promise about becoming a 'great nation.' I want a SON!"

Abram had been waiting a long time. God had promised many descendants to Abram back when he was a mere 75 years old (12:4). He would be 100 years old when Isaac was finally born (21:5). That means Abram and Sarai waited 25 years for God to fulfill His promise.

We don't know how long Abram had already been waiting at this point in the story, but the Bible tells us he was 86 when Ishmael was born (16:16), so we can guess that this exchange between God and Abram occurred sometime in the first decade after God had made the promise.

How long do you patiently wait for answers to your prayers? Does a week seem too long to wait? What about a month? Waiting for a year seems to be beyond our ability. To see that Abram waited for a quarter of a century for an answer should give us hope to wait for our own prayers to be answered.

Abram could have given up. He could have decided that he didn't want to wait on God anymore. (He *did* eventually make a mess of things when he tried to fulfill God's promise on his own by having a child with Hagar.) At this point in the story, however, he chose to believe. If only he had continued to hang on to that belief.

What answer from God are you waiting for? Is it the answer to a prayer for the return of a rebellious child? Is it the answer to a prayer for the salvation of a family member? Is it the answer to a prayer for restoration in your marriage? For a job? For healing? For provision? Whatever it is, keep on praying and waiting. Release it into God's hands and let Him do it in His way and His time. His answer will be worth the wait.

⸙

Dear God, help me to have faith enough to believe You will answer my prayers. Give me the patience to wait for the answers to appear. Keep me from giving up and taking matters into my own hands. Instead, enable me to trust that You have heard my prayers and will answer in Your perfect way and time. Keep me from being anxious or impatient as I wait on You so that I don't become discouraged and stop praying. Help me to rest in Your peace during my times of waiting. In Jesus' name I pray.

10

DO NOT BE AFRAID

᠆᠆ Read and Consider ᠆᠆

Deuteronomy 1:19-30

"See, the LORD your God has given you the land. Go
up and take possession of it as the LORD, the God
of your fathers, told you. Do not be afraid; do
not be discouraged" (Deuteronomy 1:21).

Many of the people listening to these words had spent 40 long years in the desert. Their parents had stood at this very spot decades earlier, but they had let their fears overwhelm them. In punishment for that blatant lack of faith, God gave that generation a death sentence: "Not one of the men who saw my glory and the miraculous signs I performed in Egypt and in the desert but who disobeyed me and tested me ten times—not one of them will ever see the land I promised on oath to their forefathers" (Numbers 14:22-23). The nation wandered until all the rebellious people died.

That rebellious generation's children now stood poised in the same spot. And what was Moses' message to them? He recounted what had gone before. He told the story of their parents' rebellion and lack of faith. They needed to hear and understand. Would they be prone to the same fear and rebellion, or would they be different? Would they enter and possess the land in full confidence of God's promises? God said to them what He had said to their parents, "Do not be afraid; do not be discouraged."

Walking into a closer relationship with God can be like entering your own personal promised land. You know it's a good place, but it's still filled with unknowns. Following Jesus doesn't mean life is going to be easy. You'll still have giants to battle, territory to claim, and work to do. But God says regarding your journey with Him, "Do not be afraid; do not be discouraged." And the reason is because "the LORD your God, who is going before you, will fight for you" (1:30).

You see, He already knows the unknowns. He knows about the giants. He has the battle plan. All you need to do is continually look to Him in prayer and follow His lead.

Thank You, Lord, for all of the wonderful things You have done for me in the past, that You are doing for me today, and that You will do for me in the future. Keep me from fear and discouragement as I look to the challenges ahead. Thank You that You fight for me, and You strengthen me and lift me above the things that seem like giants in my life. Thank You that You go before me with a plan for battle. I look to You for guidance so I may possess all You have for me. In Jesus' name I pray.

11

GOD IS YOUR REFUGE

<small>ᴐᴔ⤳ Read and Consider ⤲ᴑᴐ</small>
Deuteronomy 33

*"There is no one like the God of Jeshurun, who rides on
the heavens to help you and on the clouds in his majesty.
The eternal God is your refuge, and underneath are the
everlasting arms...Blessed are you, O Israel! Who is like you,
a people saved by the LORD? He is your shield and helper
and your glorious sword" (Deuteronomy 33:26-27,29).*

What an amazing picture! God rides on the heavens to help you. He is your refuge. His arms are holding you up, no matter how heavy your load, how difficult your circumstances, or how strong your fears. God not only fights for you but also provides you with a safe refuge. He actually fights in your place while you rest in the safety He gives. He shields you, saves you, and gains victory for you.

As you pray, ask God to show you how this passage applies to your life right now. Think of the specific challenges you face. Picture yourself in His loving protection as He fights your battles for you. Don't try to face your challenges alone. God doesn't want that. Whenever you try to go out on your own strength, He is grieved because you are not allowing Him to do for you all that He longs to do. He is also grieved because you make yourself more vulnerable to Satan's attack. Every time you ask God for help, He will rush to your side, and the enemy will be forced to flee from you. Remember that every time the enemy attacks, the Lord is greater than anything you face in your life. Turn to Him and trust Him to show Himself strong on your behalf.

*Lord, You are great and there is no other God but You.
You are my safe refuge from the storm. Help me to find
my rest in You as You go to battle against all that opposes
me. No matter whether my battles are with finances,
relationships, health, or obedience, I know that because of
Your presence in my life, I will never face those challenges
alone. I depend on Your strength and not mine. You
are my shield and my helper. You not only protect me,
but You hide me from the enemy and help me to escape
his clutches. Thank You that You love me so much.
In Jesus' name I pray.*

12

ASK GOD *for* DISCERNMENT

Jeremiah 23:16-32

*"This is what the LORD Almighty says: 'Do not listen to
what the prophets are prophesying to you; they fill you
with false hopes. They speak visions from their own minds,
not from the mouth of the LORD'" (Jeremiah 23:16).*

Just as the Israelites centuries ago, we all long to hear directly from
God. We want to hear prophetic words of truth. We need words
of hope. Sometimes we're so desperate for it that we're willing to
listen to just about anyone who says, "God told me..." But Jeremiah
spoke about the dangers of listening to the wrong voices.

Someone claiming to speak for God must meet a very high stan-
dard—perfection! God declared that His prophets would always be
correct in their pronouncements. What they said would come true.
Any mistake would make their message null and void (Deuteronomy
18:20-22). We make a serious mistake if we describe predictions as
truly "prophetic" when they come from someone with a track record
of wild guesses and incorrect declarations.

But then, how do we know for sure whether what we are hearing
from someone is the truth?

Our first tool of evaluation is God's Word. Those who contradict
or twist what God has already declared cannot be trusted. God
says not to listen to voices that speak lies, for "they speak visions
from their own minds, not from the mouth of the LORD" (Jeremiah
23:16). Any vision for the future that is full of failure and empty of
hope is not from God (Jeremiah 29:11). And "positive" visions that

discount God's power often express someone's wishful thinking. So always check out what you hear against the teachings of Scripture.

Our second tool of evaluation is the Holy Spirit. When we are born again, the Holy Spirit comes to dwell in us. Jesus called the Holy Spirit our "Counselor" and the "Spirit of truth," promising that He would "guide you into all truth" (John 16:7,13). When in doubt about what someone is saying or teaching, always pray for the Spirit to show you the truth.

Whenever you pray, ask the Holy Spirit to give you discernment and the ability to identify what is from Him and what is not. If people are giving you advice you're not sure about, ask Him to give you revelation regarding that.

Each time you read God's Word, ask Him to speak to you through it. If you have confusion about things people have spoken to you, ask Him to show you whether their words line up with *His* Word. Don't listen to people with visions from their own minds and not from the mouth of God.

~~~~~~~

God, help me to hear Your voice speaking to my heart.
Give me discernment so I can always distinguish between
those who speak Your truth and those who give false
prophesies filled either with fear or false hope. Help me
to examine what I hear against the teaching of Your
Word. Holy Spirit, guide me in all truth just as You have
promised. Help me to identify what is from You and what
is not. Speak to my heart every time I read Your Word so
that I am never confused by things I hear. Imprint Your
Word on my heart so that I remember it at all times.
In Jesus' name I pray.

13

PRAY THAT YOUR FAITH WILL NOT FAIL

"But I have prayed for you, Simon, that your faith may not fail. And when you have turned back, strengthen your brothers" (Luke 22:32).

Jesus prayed that Peter's faith wouldn't fail. And He told Peter this in the middle of their last Passover meal together—the Last Supper—just before revealing that Peter would deny Him. Peter did fail an important test when he denied Jesus, but ultimately his faith did not fail. He could have given up and hid himself in fear and refused to follow God's call. He had denied the very Son of God, after all. But his faith wasn't in works, or perfection, or in himself; it was in Jesus. Peter went on to lead the first-century church even after his failure on the night of Christ's trial.

Jesus' prayer was answered. Peter's faith didn't fail. Jesus' prayer shows us that if our faith doesn't fail, we can endure hardship, face temptation, and even act faithlessly at times, but ultimately we can be God's instruments to do great things. Faith is like the foundation of a house. If the foundation gives way, the house will crumble. Pray that your faith will not fail so your foundation will stay solid.

Pray the same for others as well. When you don't know what to pray for someone—when that person's needs are so great or when you just can't put your finger on the problem—one of the things you can pray for is that his or her faith will not fail. In fact, that's a good prayer to pray for people any time you pray. Who among us doesn't need to have stronger faith?

Father God, I pray my faith will not fail when I am put to the test. Help me to resist doubt and fear so that my foundation will be built solidly in Christ and therefore will not crumble. Enable me to be a person who strengthens the faith of others because my faith in You is so strong. Help me to pray for others that their faith will not fail and they will refuse to fall into doubt. In Jesus' name I pray.

14

Expectant Prayer

~ Read and Consider ~

1 Kings 18:16-39

_"'Answer me, O Lord, answer me, so these people will know
that you, O Lord, are God, and that you are turning their
hearts back again.' Then the fire of the Lord fell and burned
up the sacrifice, the wood, the stones and the soil, and also
licked up the water in the trench" (1 Kings 18:37-38)._

If there is anything like instant replay in heaven, countless believers will want to watch the moment when Elijah gave the signal and God's fire fell and consumed the soggy sacrifice. Elijah had made it impossible to set the sacrifice on fire outside of a miracle from God. And a miracle is what he expected God to do. This is in great contrast to the hours of agonized pleading by the prophets of Baal, urging their mute and impotent god to send a little spark and light the fire under _their_ sacrifice.

Years earlier, Moses had warned the people that "God is a consuming fire, a jealous God" (Deuteronomy 4:24). So the way God answered Elijah's prayer was perfectly in character. God doesn't reveal all of His glory because He knows we couldn't handle it. That's why when God makes His presence known, even through messengers, His first words often are "Don't be afraid." But when it came to a showdown with Baal worshippers, God allowed His actions to announce, "Be afraid! God and His consuming fire are here!"

When you pray, do you expect God to do something because you know what He _is able_ to do? Or do you half expect to be disappointed because you doubt that God could do something so great for you? If you answered yes to the last question, ask God to give you a heart filled with faith and expectancy of the great things He will do in response to your prayers.

Dear Lord, I pray You would help me to have strong faith to believe You will do great things in response to my prayers. Your Word tells of the magnificent and miraculous things You have done for people, and I know You are the same today and in the future as You were in the past. I believe You can do magnificent and miraculous things in response to my prayers as well. Help me to know and trust You so well that I will pray big enough to allow You to do the great things You want to do through me. In Jesus' name I pray.

15

PRAISING GOD *in* GOOD TIMES *and* BAD

Read and Consider
Job 1

"At this, Job got up and tore his robe and shaved his head. Then he fell to the ground in worship and said: 'Naked I came from my mother's womb, and naked I will depart. The LORD gave and the LORD has taken away; may the name of the LORD be praised'" (Job 1:20-21).

If God is in control, then why is this happening to me? This may be your first reaction when calamity strikes. Everyone has times of suffering, some to a greater extent than others.

Suffering is unavoidable, inescapable, and often undeserved.

Job, the man who did nothing to deserve his fate, lost everything, including all of his children and his health. Life can't get worse than that. Through it all, however, and even in his greatest hour of grief, he never cursed God. He could have blamed God, but he didn't. He trusted Him instead. His reaction to the tremendous loss was to humble himself and worship God.

Job endured that terrible time without wavering in his worship of God, and his life was eventually restored. Job lost seven sons and three daughters, and in the end God gave him seven new sons and three new daughters. "The LORD blessed the latter part of Job's life more than the first" (42:12). You may be thinking, "Yes, that's nice, but Job still lost the first seven sons and three daughters. You can't just replace a child the way you can replace a house or a herd of sheep."

It's true that Job suffered greatly. But because of his attitude, God brought good out of it. Job did not blame the Lord and say, "Why did You let this happen, God?" Instead, he said that life contains good and bad situations, and we should accept each with the same amount of reverence for God. The Bible says to "consider blessed those who have persevered. You have heard of Job's perseverance and have seen what the Lord finally brought about. The Lord is full of compassion and mercy" (James 5:11). No matter what difficult time we go through, there will be a time when life is good again.

What a powerful illustration of what we should do in response to tragedy in our own lives. God gives us what we have, and He takes it away as He sees fit. We are to praise Him for all of it. We won't always know the reason for our suffering, but we can know that God allows things to happen to us for His purpose. This doesn't make our suffering any easier, but it does give us hope for the future.

Don't give up in the midst of great loss, disappointment, or failure, or you will miss the greatest miracle in your life. If instead you praise God through it, you will see the birth of something new and good.

⤜∞⋙⋘∞⤛

Dear God, Help me to praise You no matter what is happening in my life—in good times and in bad times. Even in the midst of loss, disappointment, sickness, or failure, I want to lift up praise to You because I know that every time I do, You will work powerfully in my situation. I know Your Word says that those who persevere will be blessed. Enable me to persevere no matter what challenges I face because I trust in Your love and mercy. In Jesus' name I pray.

16

RECEIVE BEAUTY *for* ASHES

⟶ Read and Consider ⟵
Isaiah 61

> *"He has sent me...to bestow on them a crown*
> *of beauty instead of ashes, the oil of gladness*
> *instead of mourning, and a garment of praise*
> *instead of a spirit of despair" (Isaiah 61:1,3).*

The Jews had plenty to grieve about. The nation had struggled for many generations with taking God at His word and following Him faithfully. The prophet Isaiah was a strong voice for God, calling His people to renewed faithfulness. And he didn't leave anyone out. Isaiah confronted the wealthy and even the royalty with their lack of commitment to God's ways. The real problem in Jerusalem was that not enough people were grieving. In fact, they were not concerned at all that they were, in essence, snubbing their noses at God.

But for those who willingly turned their faces to God and repented of their sins, Isaiah had some good news. God promised comfort for those who grieved, beauty instead of ashes, oil instead of mourning, praise instead of despair. There was hope for those who understood that the Lord's favor would come upon all who sincerely sought to love and obey Him.

Do you ever grieve over the sins of your life or your own community or nation? If so, bring your grief to God and let Him trade it for gladness. Do you ever look at the ashes of your life or the lives of others and feel that great sense of loss? If so, God wants to give you beauty in exchange.

God knows what to do with despair. So seek Him. Sit with Him. Grieve with Him. Repent before Him. Let Him renew your life.

Ask Him for beauty, gladness, and a garment of praise. Then you can say with the ancient prophet, "I delight greatly in the LORD; my soul rejoices in my God. For he has clothed me with garments of salvation and arrayed me in a robe of righteousness" (61:10).

Dear God, I grieve over my own sins and over any time I have not lived Your way. I don't know how much I must have lost, or the blessings I have forfeited, because I have lived my way. But I confess my sins of thought, word, and action to You now and ask that You would give me beauty instead of ashes, gladness instead of mourning, and a garment of praise instead of despair. I also grieve for the sins of my nation. I know there is a great price to pay for them, so I pray that You will bring Your people together to fast and pray in humble repentance before You. Help us lift up praise in unity, knowing only You can turn the hearts of people toward You.
In Jesus' name I pray.

17

PRAISE IS *the* PUREST
FORM *of* PRAYER

<small>⤛ Read and Consider ⤜</small>
Isaiah 43:6-21

*"I provide water in the desert and streams in
the wasteland, to give drink to my people, my
chosen, the people I formed for myself that they
may proclaim my praise" (Isaiah 43:20-21).*

My definition of prayer is simply *communicating with God.* It's a love relationship first and foremost. Prayer is baring your soul to the One who loved you before you even knew of Him and letting Him speak to your heart.

Far too often prayer becomes a complicated issue for people. In fact, there can seem to be so many aspects to it that people can become intimidated. They fear that they can't pray well enough, right enough, long enough, or eloquently enough. They are afraid that their prayers won't be heard because they themselves are not good enough, holy enough, or knowledgeable enough. In all the books I have written, I have sought to dispel that kind of fear and intimidation and make prayer accessible to everyone.

One of the most important forms of prayer—or *communicating with God*—is praise and worship. Worship is the *purest* form of prayer because it causes our minds and souls to focus entirely on God and away from ourselves. It communicates our love, devotion, reverence, appreciation, and thankfulness to God, exalting Him for who He is, communicating our longing for Him, and drawing close to Him for the sake of being close. When we worship God, we are the closest to Him we will ever be. That's because praise welcomes His presence in our midst.

We were created to praise God. And God wants to make praise and worship of Him a way of life. Not necessarily with a hymn and a harp, but with a song in our heart that breaks forth through our lips as praise to the One who created us, formed us, gave us life. When we walk with Him, stay in fellowship with Him, use the gifts He has given us, serve Him wherever we find ourselves, and live for Him at all times, we can't help but praise Him for who He is and all He has done. When we do that for which we were created, we connect with our purpose. It fills our souls. It sets our path right.

Make praise and worship of God the way you live your life every day, and you'll sleep in peace every night.

❦

God, I want to show my love, reverence, devotion, and
appreciation for You as I lift You up in worship. I praise
You for who You are and for all You have done in this world
and in my life. Help me to live every day with praise and
thanksgiving in my heart so that I will fulfill my greatest
purpose and calling on earth—which is to worship and
glorify You. Help me to make worshipping You a way
of life—the first and last thing I do every day, and my
immediate reaction to whatever happens in my life.
In Jesus' name I pray.

18

The POWER *of* INTERCESSION

Exodus 32:1-14

*"Then the LORD relented and did not bring on his people
the disaster he had threatened" (Exodus 32:14).*

Can prayer change God's mind? God was angry with the Israelites' disobedience, corruption, and rebellion, and He spoke
to Moses of His intent to destroy them. Moses, however, sought
God's favor and pleaded with the Lord to spare the very people He
had miraculously brought out of Egypt. Exodus 32:14 says the Lord
"relented," which means He decided not to do as He had planned.
Did Moses actually change the mind of God?

Scripture speaks again and again of the power of intercession.
The power is not in us as human beings, of course, or in the order or
frequency of the words we speak. The power comes solely from God,
the One who hears us. "The prayer of a righteous man [or woman]
is powerful" (James 5:16).

Intercession is empowered when it is based on the promises of
God. You can pray for another person, but if what you're asking is not
consistent with or contradicts His promises, your prayers won't be
effective. When your prayers for another are in line with His Word,
God *will* respond. This is another good reason to read the Bible daily.

Base your prayers on the truth of God's Word. As Moses did,
you can pray God's Word back to Him, reminding Him of what
He has promised. You can stand before God "in the gap" (Ezekiel
22:30) and intercede for the lives of others, and for your nation.
Intercession is a precious privilege. Who knows what a difference
your prayers can make?

*Lord, help me to have a greater knowledge of Your
Word so that I will always pray in alignment with
Your will. I know the power I have in prayer is Your
power working through me. Help me to never get in the
way of what You want to do in response to my prayers.
Help me to make a major difference in the lives of my
family, friends, and neighbors when I pray. Help me
to recognize where and when my prayers can make a
major difference in preventing something bad from
happening. Teach me how to intercede on behalf of others.
In Jesus' name I pray.*

19

The IMPORTANCE *of* CONFESSION

*"David was conscience-stricken after he had counted
the fighting men, and he said to the LORD, 'I have
sinned greatly in what I have done. Now, O LORD, I
beg you, take away the guilt of your servant. I have
done a very foolish thing'" (2 Samuel 24:10).*

No one had to say anything—David just *knew* it. The number
came back and his conscience immediately pricked him. He
realized that he had wanted to count his fighting men because it
would make him feel proud, make him feel powerful and in control.
But when his arrogance and illusion were revealed, David confessed
his sin to God.

When we do something we know is wrong, our conscience usually
lets us know. We feel ashamed, tortured, and terrible. But we must
be careful that Satan doesn't make us feel so condemned about our
sin that we are too ashamed to come before God. The enemy wants
us to struggle with guilt to the point that we can't even pray. But
the Lord has given us a way out of that kind of condemnation. It's
called confession.

Confessing is more than just apologizing. Anyone can do that.
We all know people who are good apologizers. The reason they are
so good at it is that they get so much practice. They have to say
"I'm sorry" over and over again because they never change their
ways. In fact, they sometimes say "I'm sorry" without ever actually
admitting to any fault. Those are the professional apologizers, and
their confessions don't mean anything. But *true* confession means

admitting in full detail what you have done, and then fully *repenting* of it. Repentance means being so deeply sorry for what you have done that you will do whatever it takes to keep it from happening again. Confession means *recognizing* we have done wrong and *admitting* our sin. Repentance means being *sorry* about our sin to the point of grief, and so we *turn* and *walk away* from that sin.

Confession and repentance do not negate consequences, however. David went to the right place and did the right thing, but he still had to pay the price. Sometimes our sin sets in motion consequences that we must handle with the Lord's help.

Anytime you feel convicted about something and you need to confess it before God, don't hesitate. The sooner you do it, the better you will feel. Also, ask God to show you any sin in your life that *needs* to be confessed. (Too often we don't even see it.) You will be amazed at how quickly God answers that prayer.

Lord, I pray You would show me any sin in my life so that I can confess it before You. I don't want guilt in my conscience to dilute my walk with You or inhibit my prayers because I am ashamed to come before You in confidence. Help me to always have a repentant heart so that I will quickly turn away from sin. Enable me to come before You with confession immediately when I feel convicted about something I have done or not done. In Jesus' name I pray.

20

BELIEVING WITHOUT SEEING

ᴄᴇᴏ Read and Consider ᴏᴇᴏ
John 20:19-29

*"Then Jesus told him, 'Because you have seen me,
you have believed; blessed are those who have not
seen and yet have believed'" (John 20:29).*

We've all known people like Thomas. People who are hard to convince, who frequently have doubt, and who are often negative. People who don't believe in what they can't see. Probably all of us have been that way ourselves at one time or another.

Even after all the other disciples believed in the resurrection because they had seen Jesus in person, Thomas still wouldn't believe *them*. He didn't believe it until Jesus appeared in the room where all of them were gathered behind a locked door. One might think that alone would be enough evidence. But Thomas still had to put his fingers on Jesus' hands where the nails had been driven though them and on His side where the spear had pierced it. Jesus told Thomas that he was only believing because he had seen it, but those who believed *without* seeing would be blessed.

Those of us who believe that Jesus died for us and was resurrected from the dead are among the blessed. But God wants to bless us in many ways that require faith. Faith in His Word. Faith in His promises. Faith in His love, power, and goodness. He wants us to believe for things we can't yet see. Thomas needed help to believe. Often we do too. And like the father who brought his son to Jesus for healing, we can cry out to God, "I do believe; help me overcome my unbelief!" (Mark 9:24).

In times of doubt, we must be honest with God. We don't want to be people who won't believe until we see it. Because when it comes to prayer, the truth is we won't see it until we believe.

~~~

Lord, I know You want to bless me in countless ways that require believing without seeing. Help me to have the kind of faith I need in order to overcome all doubt. Help me to have faith in Your Word and Your promises, and in Your love, goodness, and power. Help me to trust that You are answering my prayers even when I cannot see it. Give me strong faith in Your Word and in all Your promises to me. Enable me to believe for the things I cannot yet see.
In Jesus' name I pray.

21

It's Never Too Late *to* Turn *to* God

⤳ Read and Consider ⤳
Joel 2:12-27

"I will repay you for the years the locusts have eaten—the great locust and the young locust, the other locusts and the locust swarm—my great army that I sent among you" (Joel 2:25).

U p to this point, Joel's prophecy was gloom and doom for those who had turned their backs on God. He warned of a day of judgment coming—a day so dreadful that he asked, "Who can endure it?" Even so, Joel kept reminding the people to repent and seek God's forgiveness.

The people had sinned greatly. They had bowed to other gods and succumbed to the idolatry in the world around them. They had been far from God for a long time.

Joel says it's not too late. God would forgive and bless them if they would return to Him in prayer and repentance.

When we pray, repenting of our sinfulness, our hearts become soft toward God, and we gain a renewed vision. We see there is hope. We have faith that He will restore all that has been devoured, destroyed, and eaten away. Even years of life that have been wasted in godless living can be restored. Trust God to take away all pain, hopelessness, hardness, and unforgiveness. Have faith in His ability to resurrect love and life from the deadest of places. Understand that He wants to restore what has been lost so that you will know He is God and glorify His name.

What is broken in your life? What have the "locusts" eaten? What has been lost, destroyed, or ruined? God says He will restore it when you turn to Him. It's never too late.

Dear God, I thank You that it is never too late to turn to You and see restoration happen in my life. Even though I feel there has been time wasted when I didn't live fully for You, I pray that You would redeem the time and help me to make up for it. Restore anything that has been lost, wasted, or ruined so I can give You the glory. If there is any hardness in my heart, I pray You would soften it so that I can hear Your voice speaking to me. I open myself to Your full restoration of all that has been devoured by the enemy in my life.
In Jesus' name I pray.

22

A STREAM *of* REFRESHING

―― Read and Consider ――
Song of Songs 4

"You are a garden fountain, a well of flowing water streaming down from Lebanon" (Song of Songs 4:15).

Wouldn't it be wonderful to be thought of as a well of living water, flowing like a refreshing stream? Especially by the people around us and those closest to us in our lives. Wouldn't it be great to be loved, adored, and appreciated in the way that adoration is described in chapter 4? But that is the way God thinks about His people. He loves us with a beautiful and unfailing love.

We all want to have a committed, deep, pure, unconditional, sacrificing, heart-uniting relationship in our lives with someone who will not leave or forsake us for someone better. We all want to be thought of as spotless and flawless. We all want to be remembered as pleasing and beautiful. And that is the way God already thinks of us. He sees us through His Son, Jesus, who is all those things. And because we have received Jesus into our lives, His beauty, purity, and perfection is what God sees in us. And the more we spend time with the Lord and surrender our lives completely to His will, the more others will see *Him* in us.

The Holy Spirit flowing in us is what enables us to be a stream of refreshing for other people. All we have to do is open up to His flow in our lives by inviting His presence to fill us afresh each day. When we do, He will pour out on us His river of living water and His everlasting flow of love. That, along with the beauty of His presence in us, will be more than enough to attract others with a refreshing that will wash over their souls.

⁓∂∞⊂∞⊙⁓

Lord, fill me afresh with Your Spirit today and overflow me with Your healing stream so that when I am with anyone else, they will sense Your presence. Make me to be like a well of refreshing water flowing out to others. I know You see me through Your Son, Jesus. I pray others will also see Jesus in me, even if they don't fully understand what it is they are seeing. I know I cannot be a constant stream of refreshing to others without Your enablement. Pour in me Your river of living water so that Your love flows through me continuously. In Jesus' name I pray.

23

I Will Praise You

—~ Read and Consider ~—
Isaiah 12

*"I will praise you, O Lord. Although you were angry with
me, your anger has turned away and you have comforted
me. Surely God is my salvation; I will trust and not
be afraid. The Lord, the Lord, is my strength and my
song; he has become my salvation" (Isaiah 12:1-2).*

The Lord gets angry about sin. We must not fool ourselves by
thinking that God overlooks our sin just because He loves us, or
that we can somehow get away with sin because we're one of God's
kids. Sin is ugly. Sin caused the death of His beloved Son. Sin will
not be tolerated by our holy God.

But sin is a part of our nature. Paul wrote, "I know that nothing
good lives in me, that is, in my sinful nature. For I have the desire
to do what is good, but I cannot carry it out. For what I do is not
the good I want to do; no, the evil I do not want to do—this I keep
on doing" (Romans 7:18-19). Although we are saved from sin, we
continue to struggle with it. We've been set free from sin, but our
sin nature still rears its ugly head. Satan constantly tries to wear
us down and tempt us to sin so we can be rendered ineffective for
God's kingdom.

While sin is a reality, and God's anger at sin is a reality, so is our
good standing with God. The battle is real, but He has armed us
for the battle (Ephesians 6:10-17). We have the ultimate weapons,
which are God's Word and our praise.

The Bible says, "The angel of the Lord encamps around those
who fear him, and he delivers them" (Psalm 34:7). Whenever the

53

enemy tries to drag you into sin, use your sword, which is the Word of God, and drown the enemy out with praise. Thank God that He is the Deliverer and you are being delivered even as you praise Him.

If you ever seem to be sliding back into the very sin you've already been set free of, don't even waste time getting discouraged. Often what seems like the same old sin coming back again may be another layer surfacing that needs to come off. You're not going backward—you are going deeper. Those deep layers of bondage can hurt far worse than the earlier ones. But the deeper you go, the stronger you get, the more mature you become, the readier you are to move into all God has for you.

If you fall (and everybody does at times), remember that you have the weapon of repentance. Go to God immediately. Confess your sin and clear the air. Show Him your repentant heart. His anger will turn away, and He will comfort you (Isaiah 12:1).

Then praise God for all the glorious things He has done and is doing in your life.

❦

Lord, even though I don't always do, say, or think the right thing—and I know sin displeases You—I thank You that You always love me and will hear my confession. Give me the discernment to hide myself in You when I see temptation coming. You are my Savior and my Deliverer, and I lift up praise to You whenever I sense the enemy trying to draw me away from Your path. Help me to run to You at the first sign of trouble. Better yet, help me to live in You at all times so that trouble only causes me to praise You more.
In Jesus' name I pray.

24

GOD'S CHOSEN FAST

⤙ Read and Consider ⤚
Isaiah 58:6-14

"Is not this the kind of fasting I have chosen: to loose the chains of injustice and untie the cords of the yoke, to set the oppressed free and break every yoke?" (Isaiah 58:6).

God gives us many wonderful keys for spiritual growth—keys such as speaking and reading His Word, praise, prayer, faith, and also fasting. Don't let your life be locked up because you are not using all of your keys. Fasting is a key to total health in every part of your being.

Fasting is not the easiest of disciplines, but it's not the hardest either. If you have a disease or health problems, check with your physician to see if it is safe for you. If it is, fasting can provide an especially close time with your heavenly Father. If you can begin the discipline of fasting for even one day each month, you will feel fresh, renewed, and cleansed in body, mind, and soul. And you will experience a special fellowship with God as you deny your physical desire for food and turn your focus on God.

Fasting is a spiritual discipline that is a denial of self. When you deny yourself, you position the Lord as *everything* in your life. This breaks the bonds of oppression. It causes things to change. Deliberately denying yourself food for a set period of time in order to give yourself more completely to prayer and closer communication with God has great rewards.

There are many religions in which fasting is a regular spiritual practice. There are also many people who fast who have no religious beliefs related to fasting but want a natural cure or cleansing for the body. We, as believers in Jesus who take seriously the written Word of God, must do our fasting unto the Lord to honor, worship, and glorify Him. It is not just a religious exercise; it is a step of obedience to God for the purpose of ministering unto Him. This is a personal matter between you and God—an offering to Him—and should be approached prayerfully and by the leading of the Holy Spirit.

Fasting goes hand in hand with prayer, so always fast with the intent of praying too. Fasting is not intended to twist God's arm into getting what you want out of Him, or something you do to win His approval, but it is a time of offering your concerns to Him.

Dear God, help me to be disciplined enough to fast and pray as You would have me to. I want to deny the desires of my flesh in order to focus entirely on my desire for more of You. I want to break every yoke of oppression in my life and in the lives of others so that we see great breakthrough. I want to see the chains of injustice loosened. Untie the places where we are tied up and can't move. Thank You for Your promise that when we fast and pray, You will answer our prayers and we will find joy in You. In Jesus' name I pray.

25

CONFESSION *and* REPENTANCE

*"But the Israelites said to the LORD, 'We have sinned.
Do with us whatever you think best, but please
rescue us now.' Then they got rid of the foreign gods
among them and served the LORD. And he could
bear Israel's misery no longer" (Judges 10:15-16).*

Sin separates us from God. It is a simple truth. This passage demonstrates the process we all need to go through in order to remove that barrier and come into right relationship with Him again. The first part of the process involves confession—telling God what you have done wrong. The second part involves repentance—turning away from the wrongdoing. The Israelites confessed that they had worshipped foreign gods; then they got rid of their idols and served the Lord.

When we don't confess our sins, we end up trying to hide from God. Just like Adam and Eve in the garden, we feel we can't face Him. But the problem with attempting to hide from God is that it's impossible. The Bible says that everything we do will be made known—even the things we say and think in secret.

Nothing is heavier and more destructive than sin. We don't realize how heavy it is until we feel its crushing weight in our relationships; we don't see how destructive it is until we hit the wall it has put up between God and us. And, as the Israelites experienced, nothing is more freeing and marvelous than God's compassion and grace. When you confess your sin, you're not informing God of something

He doesn't already know. God wants to know that *you* know you've sinned and that you are ready to turn away from it.

<hr>

*Dear God, I don't want anything to separate me from You.
Nothing is worth that. I want to confess to You anything
I have done wrong and anything that is not pleasing in
Your eyes. Wherever I have bowed my heart to what You
consider an idol in my life, reveal it to me and I will confess
it, repent of it, and get rid of it. I want to serve only You.
I don't want to even think for a moment that I can ever
hide any sin from You. Help me to repent and turn away
from anything that puts up a wall between You and me.
In Jesus' name I pray.*

26

Repenting Before God *in* Prayer

1 *Chronicles* 21:1-19

> *"David said to God, 'Was it not I who ordered the*
> *fighting men to be counted? I am the one who has*
> *sinned and done wrong. These are but sheep. What*
> *have they done? O Lᴏʀᴅ my God, let your hand fall*
> *upon me and my family, but do not let this plague*
> *remain on your people'" (1 Chronicles 21:17).*

King David had many highs of faith and obedience and some real lows of sin and disobedience. How can someone with such capacity for harmony with God be guilty of such sinful actions? This episode begins with a reminder that David was a prime target of Satan. Humiliating and defeating people whom God has called seems to be a specialty of the enemy of our souls.

Satan tempted ("incited") David, and David took the bait (21:1-2). Taking a census of fighting men appealed to the king's sense of authority and power. It was a matter of sinful pride. Satan knew just where David was weakest.

By the time Joab returned with the numbers, the king realized he had sinned. To his great credit, David owned up to his sin. He took responsibility and confessed it all to God in prayer. God used this occasion to teach David an indelible lesson about responsibility: When we sin, the consequences are real and often hurt others. When a king sins, all the people suffer. God gave David a choice of consequences, each affecting both king and people. David chose to submit to God's direct punishment rather than suffer under "the hands of men" (21:13). But the effects of his choice overwhelmed David.

Seventy thousand men died from the plague. The king gained a deeper, humbler, more painful perspective on the seriousness of sin and the holiness of God. He begged God to punish him personally and spare the rest of the people. God called off the plague, and David offered sacrifices. Our last glimpse of David in this episode shows a king chastened and respectful before God, careful not to take Him for granted.

We all need to confess our sins in prayer to God. Especially the sin of pride, which we are each tempted to have. But if we include repentance and confession as part of our prayers and then ask God to help us not commit those sins again, it enables us to stay on target with God. Even though there may be hard consequences for sin we've committed, when we come before God with humble hearts, we can be forgiven and good can come out of it.

∂∾ↄ⊂∽◌

Lord, I see in Your Word the terrible results of pride. I don't want to experience that in my life, and I especially do not want to have other people suffer because of my sin. Reveal any pride in me so that I can confess and repent of it before You. Help me to always have a humble heart and to recognize my sin quickly, as Your servant David did. Better yet, make me aware of it while it is still a thought in my mind and has not yet become an action with regrettable consequences.
In Jesus' name I pray.

27

PRAYING TOGETHER *in* UNITY

_⌒ Read and Consider _⌒
1 Timothy 2:1-8

"I want men everywhere to lift up holy hands in prayer,
without anger or disputing" (1 Timothy 2:8).

God wants all of us who believe in Him to be in unity. When we are unified, we stand together to glorify Him. Because Jesus "gave himself as a ransom for *all men*" (2:6), we are unified as recipients of His salvation and messengers of His love. That means regardless of how different we are from one another, we are all brought together by His sacrifice. But we have to make a decision to stay in unity. In fact, unity is such an important part of our spiritual foundation that our spiritual growth and the effectiveness of our prayer life depend on us being in unity with one another. God wants us to be unified in our beliefs, unified in our work for Him, and unified in our prayers. That means no arguing or fighting with our brothers and sisters.

Paul urges that "requests, prayers, intercession and thanksgiving be made for everyone," meaning both those who are already followers of Jesus and those who haven't yet met Him (2:1). But sometimes we Christians quarrel among ourselves. We get caught up in unimportant debates and useless arguments. Paul encourages all Christians to pray for others "without anger or disputing" for the common goal of winning people to the Lord (2:8).

When we are selfless in our prayers, increasingly grateful for our salvation, humbled by God's amazing love for us, staunch in our belief in Christ as Savior over all, and unified in prayer with other believers, then our prayers are powerful and will bear fruit beyond measure.

*Lord, help me to find other believers who will stand with
me in prayer. Bring godly prayer partners into my life
with whom I can pray in power. Help us to be so devoted
to You that we maintain a oneness of the Spirit, even if
we disagree on certain things. I pray we will be unified
in our belief in Your Word so that we will be unified
in our prayers. Your Word says that we are to "lift
up holy hands in prayer, without anger or disputing"
(1 Timothy 2:8). I submit my heart to You and ask You
to fill it with Your love, peace, humility, and compassion
so that I will always be the one who brings unity.
In Jesus' name I pray.*

28

The POWER of PRAISE

~~~ Read and Consider ~~~
Genesis 35:1-15

"Then come, let us go up to Bethel, where I will build an altar to God, who answered me in the day of my distress and who has been with me wherever I have gone" (Genesis 35:3).

How often do you take the time to remember what God has done for you and thank Him for it? Too often we are so busy that we accept the blessings God gives us as we rush through our hectic days without even stopping to notice them. Deadlines, meetings, and family commitments all crowd out the time we have to praise God. So often we only stop to talk to Him when we need something or when circumstances bring us face-to-face with our own inadequacy.

In this passage, however, Jacob was deliberately taking the time to slow down, stop, and build an altar to the Lord—not to ask for something—but to remember what God had done for him. And this kind of praise has power in it. When we praise God, He renews our strength and reminds us of the truth about who He is and what He wants to do in our lives. When we remember how He has been faithful in the past, it gives us confidence that we can put our trust in Him for our future. When you look back and see His hand guiding your life up to this point, it gives you faith to believe that even though the future is unclear, you can trust that He will not leave you.

It is so important to take time to reflect upon what God has done in your life and how He has been faithful to you. Then you will not fear the future, but anticipate it with the knowledge that God will be with you wherever you go.

*Almighty God, I worship You for who You are. I thank
You for all You have done for me. You have given me
strength, power, provision, and purpose. I know I need not
fear the future because I see how You have blessed me and
protected me in the past. I pray You will always be with
me to guide me in the way I should go. Help me to always
praise You as my first response to everything that happens.
In Jesus' name I pray.*

29

GETTING FREE *of the* BURDEN *of* SIN

Ezekiel 20:30-44

"There you will remember your conduct and all the actions
by which you have defiled yourselves, and you will loathe
yourselves for all the evil you have done" (Ezekiel 20:43).

If you have children of your own or you work with children in any
capacity, you know the importance of insisting that they admit
when they've done wrong. If a child lies or steals or cheats and is
never held accountable for his actions, he will be tempted to see
what more he can get away with the next time.

The same principle holds true for us as adults. Just as confession
and repentance are two life principles we insist upon for our children,
they are equally important for us as children of God. Unconfessed
sin puts a wall between us and God. Repentance, which literally
means "turning away and deciding not to do it again," is manifested
when we say, in effect, "I did this, I'm sorry about it, and I'm not
going to do it again." If sin is not confessed and repented of in that
way, we can't be free of the bondage that goes along with it.

King David knew all about unconfessed sin when he wrote,
"When I kept silent, my bones wasted away through my groaning all
day long...Then I acknowledged my sin to you and did not cover up
my iniquity. I said, 'I will confess my transgressions to the LORD'—
and you forgave the guilt of my sin" (Psalm 32:3,5).

What God said to the Israelites who disobeyed Him and didn't
repent was that they would remember their evil and hate themselves for it. We all have experienced that sense of shame when we
remember some words we've said or actions we've done that we now

deeply regret. But even though we may never forget those things, we can still be set free from the bondage and the burden of guilt by confessing and repenting of those sins. This allows God to take away the burden and make us new.

Lord, I don't want to look back over my life—even as recently as yesterday—and feel bad about myself because of the things I have done wrong. Help me to quickly recognize and confess sin. Enable me to live in such a way that I don't have regret over my words, thoughts, or actions. Help me to fully repent so that You will fully lift the burden of sin from me. I do not understand the people I see who do evil and seem to have no conscience about it. Enable my heart to be always soft toward You and loathing of sin—especially my own. In Jesus' name I pray.

30

The PROMISE *of a* FRESH START

─── ❧ Read and Consider ❧ ───
Ezekiel 18

*"Rid yourselves of all the offenses you have committed,
and get a new heart and a new spirit. Why will
you die, O house of Israel?" (Ezekiel 18:31).*

How do we get rid of each and every transgression from our lives? How can we divest ourselves of those sins of which we're not even aware? How do we get free of attitudes and actions we don't yet even recognize as being wrong? The answer is to ask God for it.

Scripture teaches that none of us is perfect. "All have sinned and fall short of the glory of God" (Romans 3:23). Because of our fallen nature, we need to ask God to bring to light any hidden sins that have taken root in our hearts so they can be dealt with now rather than later, when the consequences may be far more serious. God will do that, for "He knows the secrets of the heart" (Psalm 44:21). We've all heard stories of the "nice, likeable man" who beats his wife, abuses his children, or goes on a killing spree. You can be sure that he was a man who had hidden sin in his heart. We can be just as sure that any hidden sin in us will eventually display itself in an undesirable way. The time to catch it is now. "Turn away from all your offenses; then sin will not be your downfall" (Ezekiel 18:30). Ask God to bring any hidden sin to light so there won't be a physical or emotional price to pay for it.

Sin leads to death, but repentance leads to life. "For the wages of sin is death, but the gift of God is eternal life" (Romans 6:23). We don't confess our sins in order for God to know about them. He already knows. Confession is a chance for us to clear the slate.

Repentance is an opportunity for us to start over. We need to do both! We need a new heart and a new spirit. We need a fresh start—today and every day.

***

Lord, I pray You would take away everything in my heart that is not right before You. Help me to be rid of bad attitudes and wrong thinking. Show me anything that has taken root in my heart that should not be there so that I can free myself of it before there is a serious price to pay. Help me clear the slate and begin again with a new heart and a right spirit, just as You have spoken of in Your Word. Enable me to rid myself of all offenses against You so that sin will never be my downfall.
In Jesus' name I pray.

31

A WALK *in the* GARDEN

"Then the man and his wife heard the sound of the
LORD God as he was walking in the garden in the cool
of the day, and they hid from the LORD God among
the trees of the garden. But the LORD God called
to the man, 'Where are you?'" (Genesis 3:8-9).

Certain places just feel like this first garden. Something about the lush vegetation, the time of day, or the sounds of nature all provoke an almost overwhelming longing in us to experience what Adam and Eve enjoyed every day—a walk with God.

The world is still a wonderful setting in which to know God, but something has changed. It changed way back there, in the garden. The first two people gave up the pleasure of God's company for their own interests. They heard the sound of God walking in the garden, looking for them, wanting to enjoy their usual walk. But they had sinned. Guilt overwhelmed them. They were ashamed to see God. They lost the close relationship they had with Him, and we've struggled to recapture that closeness ever since.

God didn't hide from man; it was the other way around. Adam and Eve ducked into the bushes in shame, fear, and rebellion. But God came looking. He knew where they were, but He wanted them to know He was willing to seek their company. He was aware of their disobedience, but kept His appointment with them anyway.

What amazing fellowship they forfeited! What peace they lost! And yet, before we criticize them, remember how easily and how often we repeat their mistake. We make choices that draw us away from God. We experience overwhelming moments of His presence that we wish we could wrap up and keep; yet hours later we turn our backs on Him, trying to shut His gentle whisper out of our lives.

The power in our prayer life flows out of God's presence with us. It's not *our* power; it's *His*. We don't experience or witness that power if we insist on our agenda and our schedules. We have to plan and hold sacred the places and times when we meet God. If we don't deliberately build our lives around these "garden walks" with the Lord, the world will rapidly and relentlessly fill our hours with other commitments. As He did with Adam and Eve, God will come looking for us. But how much better would it be if He found us waiting expectantly? I don't want Him to have to call out, "Where are you?" to me. What about you?

Lord, I want more than anything to have a close walk with You. Help me not to forfeit that wonderful intimacy by being drawn toward the distractions of this world. Enable me to hear Your voice calling me so that I will answer without even a moment's delay. Help me to never hide from You for any reason. Help me to keep my heart and mind clean in Your eyes so that I never have any reason to try and hide or run from Your presence. In Jesus' name I pray.

32

EVEN WHEN WE DON'T DO
EVERYTHING RIGHT

⤞ Read and Consider ⤝
2 Chronicles 30:1-20

*"Although most of the many people who came from Ephraim,
Manasseh, Issachar and Zebulun had not purified themselves,
yet they ate the Passover, contrary to what was written. But
Hezekiah prayed for them, saying, 'May the LORD, who is
good, pardon everyone who sets his heart on seeking God—
the LORD, the God of his fathers—even if he is not clean
according to the rules of the sanctuary.' And the LORD heard
Hezekiah and healed the people" (2 Chronicles 30:18-20).*

Hezekiah had a heart like Jesus. Over and over again, Jesus broke
the religious rules of His day. He understood that God's heart
was bigger than any set of rules, even the ones meant to govern
worship and holiness. Hezekiah's prayer revealed the same thing
in him.

The people had come from far and wide to feast and worship. But
some were not prepared. They were ceremonially unclean. Hezekiah
realized, however, that what was happening—the reinstitution of
the Passover, the most important national and spiritual ritual—was
much larger than any rule regarding that ritual. If Hezekiah hadn't
realized that, the festival would have caused division rather than
unity. The work of God would have moved backward rather than
forward. The whole point of the feast would have been missed—the
point being that God saves His people based on His mercy, love,
and the blood of a lamb.

Hezekiah's prayer showed how much he believed that God would be gracious and merciful to overlook imperfection and help His children worship Him. He healed them even though they had not done everything right.

Don't hesitate to come to God. Don't be afraid to ask God to help you honor and worship Him, even when you don't do everything perfectly. He will enable you to do that.

❧❦❧

God, I thank You that even when I don't do everything right, You see in my heart the desire to do so, and You bless me with answers to my prayers. I am grateful You look past my imperfections and see the perfect qualities of Your Son, Jesus, stamped on my heart instead. Help me to live Your way so that my ways are pleasing in Your sight. Thank You that You are the God of love and mercy, and You hear my prayers when I cry to You for mercy to overlook my imperfections and help me always do the right thing. In Jesus' name I pray.

33

KNOWING WHICH WAY *to* GO

Read and Consider
Isaiah 30:19-26

"Whether you turn to the right or to the left, your
ears will hear a voice behind you, saying, 'This
is the way; walk in it'" (Isaiah 30:21).

We pray about a lot of things—things we need, things we want, safety for our families, traveling mercies, strength in times of grief. Very often, we pray for guidance. We need to know God's will about a big decision, how to solve a problem, how to deal with people, how to face adversity. We want to know God's will because it is a place of safety. When we live outside of God's will, we forfeit His protection.

We all want to be in the center of God's will. That's why we shouldn't pursue a career, move to another place, or make any major life change without knowing that it is the will of God. The way we find out is to regularly ask God to show us what His will is and then ask Him to lead us in it. When you ask Him to speak to your heart, He will do that. He will give you peace about a certain thing and *lack* of peace about others. What joy to have peace that as we confidently set foot in a certain direction, God is leading us on that particular path. We can be confident that whatever happens along the way, we don't have to worry because we are right where God wants us to be.

But all too often we don't hear that voice behind us. We hear the voices clamoring around us instead; we hear our own internal concerns and issues; we're in a hurry, and so we just forge ahead on the path and hope that everything will work out in the end.

73

When Isaiah gave this promise of God's guidance, it was in the midst of a description of people turning their hearts back to God. He had just prophesied to them about God's compassion in waiting for them to get their priorities in line. When they established right priorities, when their hearts were drawn in the right direction, God's voice would guide them.

As you seek guidance, listen for God's voice. It will be there. Take a few quiet moments to wait on Him and give Him time to respond.

⁓⁓⁓

Lord, speak to me about Your will for my life so that I can always walk in it. Your will is a place of safety and protection for me, and I need to know I am headed in the right direction. Help me to hear Your voice speaking to my heart telling me what to do, especially with regard to the decisions I need to make each day of my life. Enable me to hear Your quiet voice saying, "This is the way; walk in it" (Isaiah 30:21). Keep me from ignoring Your voice because I am unsure it is really You. Give me the discernment I need. In Jesus' name I pray.

34

GOD HEARS OUR PRAYERS
and SEES OUR HEART

∽ Read and Consider ∽
1 Peter 3:8-12

*"For the eyes of the Lord are on the righteous and his
ears are attentive to their prayer, but the face of the
Lord is against those who do evil" (1 Peter 3:12).*

Have you ever wondered if God is really listening when you pray?
If so, you're not alone. All of us have had that same question
in our minds at one time or another. We pray about a specific thing,
and if nothing happens we wonder why we are praying at all.

When Peter wrote about God's attentive ears, he was quoting
Psalm 34, a psalm written by David after he escaped with his life
from the clutches of King Saul. David then traveled to a foreign land
to seek asylum, but once he was in the court of the foreign king,
he realized he had a reputation as someone who could threaten the
king's authority. If this foreign king felt threatened (as Saul had),
David would once again be running for his life. To free himself from
this situation, David pretended to be crazy until the king literally
threw him out of the city (1 Samuel 21). After such a shrewd escape,
David wrote the psalm Peter quoted in this New Testament letter.
David celebrated the fact that when he cried out to the Lord, God
heard him. "I sought the LORD, and he answered me; he delivered
me from all my fears...This poor man called, and the LORD heard
him; he saved him out of all his troubles...The eyes of the LORD are
on the righteous and his ears are attentive to their cry...The righteous
cry out, and the LORD hears them; he delivers them from all their

troubles. The LORD is close to the brokenhearted and saves those who are crushed in spirit" (Psalm 34:4,6,15,17-18).

David's life was not easy. He went through horrible heartbreak, devastating loss, and extremely troubling situations. But through it all, he knew he was not alone. He knew that in every situation, God was there listening and answering.

We can know that too. We can have the same certainty that God not only hears our requests, He hears our heart. We may say something like, "Lord, help me get this job," but He will hear, "I'm desperate for a change. I feel so unimportant here." We may say, "God, please keep me safe," but He hears, "I am afraid of how dangerous, precarious, and out of control life seems right now." God not only hears what we want, He also knows what we need.

∽∾∿∘⊃⊂∘∾∽

> *Dear God, I thank You that You see my heart and*
> *hear my prayers. How grateful I am that when You see*
> *me, You see the righteousness of Jesus in me and not the*
> *sinner I was before I received Him into my life. Thank*
> *You that You not only hear my prayers, but You see*
> *my need and will answer the cries of my heart. I know*
> *that Your Word says You are against evildoers, but*
> *You hear the prayers of those who are righteous. Help*
> *me to do good and not evil all the days of my life.*
> *In Jesus' name I pray.*

35

The COST of FORGIVENESS

Read and Consider
Leviticus 1:1-13

*"He is to lay his hand on the head of the burnt
offering, and it will be accepted on his behalf to
make atonement for him" (Leviticus 1:4).*

In the Old Testament system of sacrifices, forgiveness came at a
price—a literal, hands-on, obvious price.

Today we understand forgiveness as we look at Christ's sacrifice.
He was our once-and-for-all payment for sin. In the Old Testament,
under the law of Moses, the people looked ahead to Christ's salvation.
With the Old Testament sacrifices and offerings, they actually *pre-
enacted* the provision that was to come through Jesus. The sacrifices
were symbols—the lives of innocent animals were offered as payment
for the sins of the people. But the people didn't simply drop a suitable
animal to be sacrificed at the door of the tabernacle. They took part
in the death of the animal. Leviticus 1:4 says that the worshipper
put his hand on the head of the animal that was to be killed. Once
the animal was slaughtered, *then* the priests handled the rest. The
animal's death symbolized the penalty for sin and the people's need
for forgiveness in order to be in a relationship with God.

When you go before God to confess your sins and accept His
forgiveness, is the price Jesus paid real to you? Is it as real as if you
put your hand on Jesus' head as He bore the cross to Golgotha?
Today, forgiveness can seem so sanitized, like the meat we buy at
the market, wrapped and labeled. We can easily forget that a death
occurred in order for us to have the provision.

Keep in mind that the price for your forgiveness was paid out of Jesus' sacrifice. The old sacrificial system gives us an effective reminder that the price was life itself.

Dear Lord, help me to never forget the great price You paid so that I could be forgiven. I don't want to ever take for granted the sacrifice You made on my behalf so that no further sacrifice of life needs to be made. Now the sacrifice I want to make is one of thanksgiving and praise to You for all that You have done to set me free from the consequences of my own sin. Thank You, Jesus, that You have made atonement for me once and for all by paying the price with Your own life. Thank You that You died the death I should have died so that I can live forever with You. In Your name I pray.

36

Praying *for* Those Who Have Hurt You

"So Moses cried out to the LORD, 'O God, please heal her!'" (Numbers 12:13).

The two people God gave to Moses to help him lead the Israelites out of slavery were his own sister and brother, Miriam and Aaron (see Micah 6:4). You'd think they would be Moses' most ardent supporters. Ironically, however, the opening verse of Numbers 12 tells us that these two family members who should have been most loyal to Moses were speaking out against him.

Family divisions wound us deeply. Friends or colleagues may hurt us, but when betrayal arises from within our own family, the pain is profound. But Moses didn't hang on to any hurt he may have felt. Instead he prayed for his sister.

God confronted both Miriam and Aaron at the Tent of Meeting, but it was upon Miriam that the discipline fell. Since Miriam's name appears before Aaron's, we can assume that she was older and that God was holding her responsible for the division she and Aaron were spreading in the camp because of their critical tongues. As a result, she was afflicted with leprosy, a horrible contagious skin disease that would cause her to be separated from the rest of the camp—perhaps for the remainder of her life. Her younger brother Aaron was horrified when he witnessed the result of their disobedience and disloyalty; he asked Moses to forgive them for their foolishness and sin.

Moses did not hesitate but immediately cried out to the Lord on behalf of his sister: "O God, please heal her!" Though Miriam still had to face the consequence of displeasing the Lord, she was restored to the people after a seven-day time-out. God responded to Moses' plea on behalf of the very one who had wronged him.

Do you have a family member who has hurt you? Have you been able to forgive that person? If not, ask God to help you forgive completely. Then pray for that person because prayer has great power to restore broken family relationships. In the process of praying, you'll begin to sense love growing in your heart for the one who hurt you. God will still hold that person accountable for the sins he or she has committed, but forgiving and praying for that person has the power to free you from all pain and bitterness. Try it and discover the wonderful freedom waiting for you when you forgive.

*Lord, I pray You would help me to forgive anyone who
has hurt me. I pray this especially concerning family
members or friends who I feel have betrayed me. Enable
me to forgive them so completely that I don't hesitate
to pray for their greatest blessing. Deliver me from
any bitterness, and help me to live in the freedom of a
forgiving heart so that there is complete reconciliation
between us. I don't want to experience the terrible
consequences of unforgiveness in my life. I don't want
to hesitate to pray for the healing or blessing of someone
because my heart is holding on to a grudge against
them. Teach me to pray for those who hurt me.
In Jesus' name I pray.*

37

FINDING PEACE *in the* MIDST *of* SUFFERING

∽ Read and Consider ∽
Job 26

*"And these are but the outer fringe of his works; how
faint the whisper we hear of him! Who then can
understand the thunder of his power?" (Job 26:14).*

God's power and ways are immeasurable, far beyond our comprehension. We will never fully understand them this side of heaven. We don't understand His ways that allow us to suffer. And we don't understand His power to redeem and restore us. That's why we must praise God no matter what is happening in our lives. We should praise Him even in the midst of suffering because it strengthens us and refines our faith in Him. Trials, hardships, and pain all serve to strengthen not only the individual, but also a society or nation. How much more should we praise God when we know for certain that God loves us, has a purpose, and is working out His plan through our every experience.

Our suffering can be compared to the refining process of silver. The heat is turned up, and as the impurities rise to the surface they are skimmed away by the refiner. Because God is sovereign, nothing that happens to us surprises Him. And as difficult as it is to accept sometimes, God even allows us, His children, to suffer.

It is in those times of suffering that we may feel as if we're on a roller coaster, vacillating up and down as we wonder why God would allow us to endure such pain. Yet if we draw close to Him, we will have a sense of peace, knowing He is in control of the situation. In spite of all that Job went through, he never doubted God's unlimited power. Job said that God's power terrified him (23:15-16). He said, when referring to God's ability to calm a raging storm, "These are but the outer fringe of his works" (26:14).

So even in the midst of turmoil and grief, praise God for the path He has chosen for you and for His refining power and love. When the heat is on, allow the Refiner to purify your soul.

Almighty God, Your power is beyond comprehension. I can't begin to understand the far-reaching greatness of Your restoration and redemption in my life. Help me to never doubt You and Your ability to restore and redeem me. Enable me to have such unwavering faith in the midst of difficult times that I rest in peace, knowing You will take care of all I care about. In the times I go through suffering and pain, help me to draw close to You, trusting You are in control of my life and empowering my prayers. In Jesus' name I pray.

38

RISING UP *out of the* DARKNESS

*"Do not gloat over me, my enemy! Though I have
fallen, I will rise. Though I sit in darkness, the
LORD will be my light" (Micah 7:8).*

No one is perfect. The people of Judah knew this very well—they had failed God miserably. And to make matters worse, their enemies were laughing at them.

Being good can be a daily struggle for many people. Our human nature is instinctively selfish, causing us to strive to satisfy our own desires. Yet God has given us His Word and His Spirit to help us combat our sinful nature. Still, we all fall into sin, some deeper than others. In those times we have a choice to make: wallow in the darkness of self-pity or repent and look to Jesus. "The LORD will be my light," wrote Micah. Sin is a dark path that first draws us in with promises of the gratification of our human desires. But when the light of the Word shines upon it, all the snares, traps, and quagmires are revealed.

Always remember that no matter how much we've failed, God is ready to forgive us when we ask Him to. He doesn't want any of His children to sink without hope of rescue. That's why He gave us His Son, Jesus, to offer us His lifeline. Reaching out in repentance is our decision. Picture a person drowning and crying out for help, when suddenly a strong arm reaches into the water. That person would obviously reach for the strong hand immediately and be saved. Confession of sin and repentance are a strong hand that reaches to us when we are drowning in our own failures, yet many people choose to reject that means of restoration. Perhaps they don't realize the danger they are in, or maybe they reject the hope offered, thinking they can save themselves. But Jesus is always there ready to pull us up and out of the darkness, no matter how deep or how many times we slip and fall.

~∂∞⊃ᴄ₆∞~

Thank You, Lord, that even if I were to fall off the path You have for me to walk, You will always be there to lift me up and put me back on it again when I repent of my sins. I thank You that even if I sink into darkness, You will be my light. I praise You as the light of my life and keeper of the flame that burns in my heart for eternity. Help me to always trust Your light in my life, and consistently be my treasure in darkness. Because of You, even though I may fall, I will rise again and worship You as the One who lights up my life. In Jesus' name I pray.

39

YOUR DAY *of* ATONEMENT

~~~ Read and Consider ~~~
Leviticus 16

"On this day atonement will be made for you, to cleanse you. Then, before the LORD, you will be clean from all your sins" (Leviticus 16:30).

The Day of Atonement, Yom Kippur, was perhaps the most important annual holy day for the ancient Jews. It was the day when the high priest entered the innermost chamber of the tabernacle (and later, the temple) to offer a sacrifice for the sins of the whole nation. The purpose of this sacrifice? The reconciliation of God and His people.

The ritual described in Leviticus 16 had several steps. It included the sacrifice of a bull and the dripping of that bull's blood onto the cover of Israel's most sacred relic—the ark of the covenant. It also included the selection of two goats. One was to be sacrificed, symbolizing the necessary payment for sin. The other goat, the scapegoat, was set free, symbolizing the sins of the people being carried into the desert.

Because of Christ's sacrifice for our sins, every day is our day of atonement. Every day we accept that His death paid for our sins. Every day our sins are carried into a desert that we will never have to enter.

In light of that reality, how do you approach God in prayer? Do you sit before God as someone God values and loves? Or do you hang your head as if you still have to earn the acceptance you've already been given? Do you rush into His presence, or do you hesitate, hoping that what the Bible teaches about His forgiveness is true. If you tend toward the latter, claim today as your day of atonement. Go to God with a heart of gratitude and thank Him that nothing stands between you and Him.

Thank You, Jesus, for paying the price for my sins so that I don't have to. Because of You, I have been reconciled to God, and I will never be separated from Him again. Thank You that every day is a day of atonement for me because of what You have accomplished on the cross as my Lord and Savior forever. Help me to extend to others the love and forgiveness You've given to me. Teach me ways I can show my gratitude to You for all You have done. In Your name I pray.

40

FINDING FORGIVENESS
THROUGH CONFESSION

∽ Read and Consider ∾
1 John 1:5-10

*"If we confess our sins, he is faithful and just
and will forgive us our sins and purify us
from all unrighteousness" (1 John 1:9).*

God offers us three steps for changing our behavior.
The first step is *confession,* which is *admitting* what we did. Everyone makes mistakes, but there is an epidemic in the world today of people who can't admit they did something wrong. God says that all we have to do is confess our sins, and He will forgive us and purify us. Confession means admitting the truth to ourselves first, then to God, and then perhaps to someone else who might have been hurt because of our sin. Sometimes we need to confess to God in front of another person who can pray for us and help us truly get our mistakes off our chest. And confession is not just admitting the truth of what we did, but it is also taking responsibility for it. To own up to wrongdoing can seem like a monumental task, but it is well worth the effort. Confession is one of the best things you can do for yourself. It cleanses your heart by releasing the burden of guilt, and it makes way for God's total forgiveness.

The second step is *repentance,* which means *being sorry* about what we did and wanting to never do it again. We don't confess sin with the intention of clearing the slate and then continuing on with the same sinful behavior, knowing we can just confess it all over again. True repentance means being so sorry before God that we don't ever want to disappoint Him by doing the same thing again.

The third step is *asking for forgiveness* so we can be *cleansed and released* from the consequences of what we did. John didn't say, "If we beg and plead with all of our hearts, then God will forgive us." He said in essence that God's forgiveness flows freely the moment we simply ask for it. God is always waiting and ready to forgive. He doesn't have to be coerced or cajoled. He *wants* us to live free of guilt and shame. He wants us to live in complete forgiveness because only then can we ever find total restoration in our lives.

⟨∞⟩

Lord, I confess my sins before You. Thank You that You are faithful to forgive them and to cleanse me from all the effects of them. If there is sin in my life I am not seeing, reveal it to me now so that I can confess it before You and be purified of all unrighteousness. Give me a heart that is quick to repent so that I am deeply sorry enough to never want to do it again. Thank You that You are faithful to forgive my sins the moment I confess them, and because of that I can always live in the wholeness of Your complete forgiveness. In Jesus' name I pray.

41

WHEN GOD DOESN'T ANSWER

—— Read and Consider ——
1 Samuel 28

"He inquired of the LORD, but the LORD did not answer him by dreams or Urim or prophets" (1 Samuel 28:6).

Sometimes God does not answer our prayers immediately. He may be telling us to wait; He may have another purpose in not giving a direct answer. Whatever the reason, it is always a good idea to "inquire of the Lord," and it is always a bad idea to take matters into our own hands. This is what King Saul did. So desperate was he for some kind of response that he just couldn't wait, so he went to a medium to get an answer.

When God does not answer your prayers, step back and wait. He is giving you an opportunity to trust Him in the midst of the uncertainty and ambiguity you may be feeling. The fact that Saul immediately consulted a medium—something he knew was directly forbidden by God and that he himself had outlawed—showed the shallowness of his trust in the Lord and his lack of commitment to God's ways.

What answer to prayer are you waiting for today? Have you become discouraged about it? Are you tempted to think that God is not listening to your prayers or that He doesn't care about your request? Are you thinking that maybe you need to step in and deal with the problem on your own since you haven't seen any response from God?

If so, ask God to help you to trust Him even when it is hard to do so. Ask Him to help you release the situation into His hands so

He can handle it *His way* and in *His time*. Tell Him you are thankful that He knows what to do better than you do.

～⌒⌒⌒⌒⌒～

> *God, I thank You that You always hear my prayers. Give me patience to wait for the answer to come in Your way and in Your perfect timing. Give me peace to accept Your answer—even if it is "No." Help me to never take matters into my own hands to try to make something happen that is not Your will. I trust You know what is best for me at all times. Help me to trust You to always do what is best for me. In Jesus' name I pray.*

42

WHEN GOD GIVES
SPECIFIC INSTRUCTIONS

ᴄ˞˞˞ Read and Consider ˞˞˞ᴄ
2 Samuel 5:17-25

"So David inquired of the LORD, *'Shall I go and
attack the Philistines? Will you hand them over to
me?' The* LORD *answered him, 'Go, for I will surely
hand the Philistines over to you'" (2 Samuel 5:19).*

God isn't always this direct, but He does occasionally give us
very specific instructions in answer to our prayers. If we ask
for guidance and depend on Him, He promises to lead us in the
direction that we should go (Proverbs 3:5-6). That is what He did
for David in this passage, directing him when and how to attack
and assuring him of the outcome. So often we do not think to ask
God for this kind of specific direction because we don't expect that
He will answer us. But He wants to guide our lives—even in the
small details—and the more we get in the habit of asking, the more
we will learn how to listen for His voice and discern what He is
telling us to do.

Don't be afraid to pray for guidance in specific areas of your life,
and don't get discouraged if you don't hear answers right away. It may
take some time to learn how to hear God's voice leading you. But you
will learn, and you will enjoy greater intimacy in your relationship
with God. He longs to have this closeness with you, so take Him
up on it and start asking questions! Tell Him the deepest thoughts
and feelings of your heart. He understands you more than *you* do.

Lord, I don't want to take one step or make any decision without Your leading. I know You care about even the smallest details of my life and want to guide me in the way I should go. Take away my peace if I should decide to step off the path of Your greatest blessing for my life. Help me to never stray from Your perfect will. Help me to pray as David did for specific answers and directions. And when You give those to me, enable me to follow Your leading. In Jesus' name I pray.

43

LOOKING *for a* BREAKTHROUGH?

Read and Consider
Joshua 6:1-20

"When the trumpets sounded, the people shouted, and
at the sound of the trumpet, when the people gave a
loud shout, the wall collapsed; so every man charged
straight in, and they took the city" (Joshua 6:20).

Have you ever needed a breakthrough in your life? Or some kind of deliverance? Perhaps you or your situation needed to be transformed, but you were facing a wall as high as the one surrounding Jericho. As far as you could see, there seemed to be no way through it.

The good thing about knowing that you need much more than your own strength in order to break down the walls in your life is that it forces you to rely on the power of God to set you free. And His deliverance and freedom are always far beyond what we can imagine. God wants you to depend on Him and His power whenever you face obstacles in your life. So each time you find that you can't seem to move beyond something you are facing, determine to go deeper into God's Word. Commit to even more fervent prayer. Decide to give God heartfelt worship regardless of what is happening.

Those three steps of obedience are powerful and will destroy whatever is standing in the way of your moving into all God has for you.

The Israelites walked around the city of Jericho 13 times in one week. So don't just stand looking at the walls that are obstructing you. Start encircling them with shouts of praise today and every day for as long as it takes.

Father God, I depend on You to help me overcome the obstacles in my life. Teach me to speak Your Word in power as I cover each situation in prayer. I lift up praise to You in the face of impossible circumstances because You are the God of the impossible. No matter what comes against me, Your power is more than enough to break through it to victory. Help me to walk around the walls that are obstructing me, while lifting up joyful praise to You, until I see them collapse. In Jesus' name I pray.

44

The POWER *of* PRAISE-FILLED GIVING

~~~ Read and Consider ~~~
1 Chronicles 29:1-20
---

*"Wealth and honor come from you; you are the ruler of all
things. In your hands are strength and power to exalt and
give strength to all. Now, our God, we give you thanks,
and praise your glorious name" (1 Chronicles 29:12-13).*

David's life was winding down, and he wanted to pave the way
for his son's reign and for the construction of the great temple.
He arranged for vast sums of raw materials to be stockpiled for the
project. As one of his last official gestures as king, David announced
he would add his own personal gift from out of his treasures as the
king. He challenged others to give in the same spirit, out of honor to
God. "Now," he said, "who is willing to consecrate himself today to
the LORD?" (29:5). Other leaders stepped up and gave. The resulting
offering provided much of the funding for the construction of the
temple.

The people were amazed at their own generosity. King David
was deeply touched by their giving and lifted up one of the greatest
prayers of praise in the Bible. It wasn't a long prayer, but every word
exalted God and recognized Him as the ultimate supplier of all
things. What more appropriate way to acknowledge God as the head
over all and the owner of everything than by contributing generously
to the building of a grand temple that would honor Him? What
better way to show trust in God's future faithfulness than to give
from the abundance of His present faithfulness?

After King David gave his personal treasure and praised God, he
acknowledged the profound effect he had felt as the people gave their

offerings. And he fervently prayed that this spirit of generosity and trust would always be a hallmark of God's people. David concluded by urging the people to "Praise the LORD your God" (29:20). They gave to God from their earthly treasures as well as giving praise to Him from their whole hearts.

Powerful prayer includes lavish praise to God for His generosity. It also includes giving to God out of a praise-filled heart. To do otherwise reveals that we revere our possessions more than our God, who has given us all that we have.

Heavenly Father, I thank You and praise You for all You have given me. Help me to give back to You with the same heart of praise I have when I receive from You. I want to be a cheerful giver. Help me to never value my possessions more than I value You and Your laws. Enable me to give the way You want me to. I know that all I have comes from You. Help me to give as You direct me and in a way that pleases You.
In Jesus' name I pray.

45

Praying *for* Success

∞ Read and Consider ∞
Genesis 24:1-27

*"Then he prayed, 'O LORD, God of my master
Abraham, give me success today, and show kindness
to my master Abraham'" (Genesis 24:12).*

When you face a big job or an important responsibility, you want to succeed. The best way to see success is to go directly to God, who wants the very best for your life, and ask for His guidance. That's what Eliezer did.

Abraham had asked his servant to find the right bride for his son Isaac. This was most likely Eliezer, Abraham's trusted servant for many years. Eliezer realized the great weight of the responsibility he carried, so he submitted the matter directly to God rather than depend solely on his own wisdom or on pure luck. He asked God for a sign, and God granted his request almost instantly. Before Eliezer had even finished praying, Rebekah arrived and offered to give him water for both himself and his camels. What a remarkable answer to prayer!

But let's go a little deeper. Who was Eliezer? If we go back to where he is named in Genesis 15:2-3, we discover that not only was he Abraham's trusted servant, but at that point, he stood to inherit all of Abraham's wealth if Abraham had no son. So not only did he lose out when Isaac was born, but Eliezer also had to find a suitable bride for Isaac. A lesser man might have been bitter about all he had lost. A lesser man might have defined "success" as doing whatever it might take to get back into that place of honor in order to gain the inheritance. A lesser man might not have cared what kind of bride he brought back to Isaac. Not Eliezer. He was determined to do the job well, so he prayed for success in the task.

God cares about your responsibilities. He wants to see you do well, to succeed. So don't be afraid to ask for success. Always keep in mind, however, that He may define success very differently than you do. Like Eliezer, walk so close to God that you're able to put aside what you might want for yourself in order to succeed at what God wants for you.

~~~

Heavenly Father, I pray for success in all I do. Guide me in everything. Show me where I have proceeded with something without first inquiring of You. Enable me to understand Your measure of success and not try to impose my own. My goal is to serve You, knowing that any success I have will be achieved only by walking perfectly in Your will. I ask for success today—in staying in Your will, in obeying what You have told me to do, and in serving You with my whole heart. In Jesus' name I pray.

46

The QUICKSAND of TEMPTATION

∽ Read and Consider ∾
2 Samuel 11

"One evening David got up from his bed and walked around on the roof of the palace. From the roof he saw a woman bathing. The woman was very beautiful, and David sent someone to find out about her" (2 Samuel 11:2-3).

K ing David was a good man. A man after God's own heart. But one night he wasn't where he was supposed to be, and he wasn't doing what he was supposed to be doing. He was supposed to be fighting with his army. Instead, he was up on his roof watching the *married* lady next door take a bath. Then he sent for her to come to his palace...and the story goes downhill from there.

You're probably familiar with it. The beautiful woman, Bathsheba, ended up pregnant, and her husband ended up conveniently dead on the front line of David's battle, being sent there specifically for that purpose by David. The king married Bathsheba, but they lost their baby. And, amazingly, had it not been for a confrontation with the prophet Nathan, David may have come out of the situation thinking he had pulled one over on God just because he had covered his tracks. But that's not how it works.

What could have saved David from the temptation to involve himself with another man's wife? Instead of feasting his eyes on that naked woman, he should have turned his eyes away, admitted his temptation to God *immediately*, and gone right into the privacy of his own room. There he could have done what he had done in the midst of so many other battles or personal struggles—fallen on his face before God in prayer, praise, and worship. If he had stayed there before the Lord until the grip of temptation had released him, these tragedies would have never happened.

But he didn't. David "sent someone to find out about her." He stuck his toe into the quicksand of temptation, and before he knew it, he was in over his head.

All of us face temptation at one time or another. It may not be the same kind that David faced, but anything that draws us away from God and entices us to do what is against God's laws is temptation. Whenever that happens to you, immediately get before God and confess it. Ask Him to set you free from it and help you do the right thing. Then worship God until you feel the temptation broken over you.

The ability to withstand temptation begins the moment you look to your Savior and Deliverer for help.

⌒⌒⌒⌒⌒

*Dear God, I pray You will help me to always successfully
resist temptation from the moment I am confronted with
it. Help me to draw closer to You when anything tries
to draw me away from You. Deliver me from the trap
of temptation before I fall into it. Give me the strength,
wisdom, and knowledge I need to fully resist temptation
the moment it presents itself. I don't want any lack of
judgment or weakness on my part to draw me away
from You and the safety and peace of Your perfect will.
In Jesus' name I pray.*

47

BE CAREFUL WHAT
YOU ASK FOR

―∽ Read and Consider ∾―
1 Samuel 8

*"So all the elders of Israel gathered together and came to
Samuel at Ramah. They said to him, 'You are old, and your
sons do not walk in your ways; now appoint a king to lead
us, such as all the other nations have'" (1 Samuel 8:4-5).*

You can probably recall times in your life when you have prayed for
something that, looking back, could have led to disaster. Although
we think we know what is best for our lives and our futures, often
we pray for the very things that would lead to our own destruction.
God knows this; He sees the big picture. He wants us to bring our
prayers into alignment with His will. In the case of the Israelites,
no amount of instruction—even from the Lord Himself through
Samuel—could convince them that they were praying amiss. So the
Lord finally gave them the king they begged for, though He knew
he would eventually be a burden to them.

Today you have the Holy Spirit to guide you, even in your praying.
So always ask the Lord to help you pray according to His will for your
life. Also seek wisdom from the Bible so you can pray in alignment
with His will. Just as Jesus did in the garden of Gethsemane, pray
"not my will, but yours be done" (Luke 22:42). This allows God to
work in your heart so you can accept His will, even if it is not what
you thought you wanted. God knows what is best for us—and we
must trust Him completely on this.

*Help me, Holy Spirit of God, to pray according to Your
will. Speak to me as I read Your Word so that I can
grow in understanding. Enable me to pray in power
regarding what pleases You. Thank You for the times
I prayed for something and You didn't give it to me
because it would not have been good. I can see that now,
and I am grateful. Help me to bring my prayers into
alignment with Your purpose and plans for my life.
In Jesus' name I pray.*

48

The POWER *to* FIGHT TEMPTATION

∽ Read and Consider ∾
Mark 1:9-13

"He was in the desert forty days, being tempted by Satan. He was with the wild animals, and angels attended him" (Mark 1:13).

How often is the word *temptation* used lightly? We might comment on some food that looks particularly "tempting," or we laughingly say we're "yielding to temptation" when we buy something we want but don't absolutely need.

Most often, however, temptation is not a laughing matter. When we crave, desire, or are enticed by something that is wrong for us, we are experiencing temptation in its most dangerous form. The Bible says we have an enemy, Satan, who would like nothing more than to tempt us to sin and destroy our lives.

Jesus knew what it was to experience temptation. Immediately following His baptism, Jesus was led into the desert by the Holy Spirit where He was tempted by Satan for 40 days. God allowed this time of testing in Jesus' life, but it was Satan who did the tempting (Matthew 4:1-11).

Even though Jesus was God incarnate, He was also fully human. How could any human being withstand a full 40 days of intensive satanic attack? Based on what Scripture relates of the life of Christ and His regular habit of spending time alone with God, we know that Jesus did not enter this grueling time of temptation unprepared. Prayer and His knowledge of the Scriptures girded Him for battle. We should strive to be like Him in our preparation for enemy attacks.

The best time to pray about temptation is *before* you fall into it.

After the lure presents itself, resisting temptation becomes much more difficult. The model prayer Jesus taught us to pray as a matter of course is a good place to start. "Lead us not into temptation, but deliver us from the evil one" (Matthew 6:13). We can also prepare to do as Jesus did and rebuke the enemy with God's Word. That means we must read it enough to know what it says. In addition to that, we can call on the Lord. "Because he himself suffered when he was tempted, he is able to help those who are being tempted" (Hebrews 2:18).

None of us is immune to temptation. We might think that as we mature in the Lord, temptation will be less intense. But the truth is, we must continue to watch out for subtle temptations and ask God to give us discernment. Never hesitate to cry out to God when you are tempted. The temptation is not the sin. Whether we sin or not has to do with whether we *entertain* the temptation or turn to God immediately. God is not only able to help us stand strong against temptation, but He can also deliver us out of it.

Lord Jesus, equip me to resist all temptation from the enemy. Enable me to be so prepared before temptation happens that I recognize the enemy's tactics from the moment they manifest. Teach me to rebuke the enemy by having a great knowledge of Your Word. Enable me to resist entertaining temptation for even a moment, but rather to turn to You immediately so that I can stand strong. Just as You resisted temptation from the enemy in the wilderness, help me be prepared for any enemy attack by being fortified by Your Word. In Your name I pray.

49

FINDING FREEDOM FROM
WHAT KEEPS YOU BOUND

ఒ∽ Read and Consider ∾ఒ

Mark 9:14-32

*"He replied, 'This kind can come out
only by prayer'" (Mark 9:29).*

Jesus' disciples attempted to exorcise a demon from an afflicted boy, but they failed. After Jesus responded to the frantic father's plea for help, the demon left the child and the disciples were left bewildered. Why had Jesus succeeded where their sincere efforts had not?

Jesus said that prayer was the key to releasing this person from bondage to satanic forces. Some manuscripts include fasting along with prayer. Fasting always increases the power of our prayers. The disciples had apparently not prepared themselves well enough by praying and fasting first.

In Matthew 18:18, Christ taught, "Whatever you bind on earth will be bound in heaven, and whatever you loose on earth will be loosed in heaven." God gives us His authority on earth. When we call on that authority, God releases power to us from heaven. Because it's God's power and not ours, we become the vessel through which His power flows. When we pray, we bring that power to bear on the situation, allowing the power of God to work through our powerlessness. When we pray, we are humbling ourselves before God and saying, "I need Your presence and Your power, Lord. I can't do this without You." When we don't pray, we are in effect saying that we have no need of anything outside of ourselves.

If you are facing a difficult situation within your own life, you have authority in the name of Jesus to stop evil and permit good. You can submit to God in prayer whatever bondage controls you—such as alcoholism, addiction, laziness, depression, infirmity, abusiveness, confusion, anxiety, fear, or failure—and fast and pray to be released from it. God will set you free.

Lord, I see in Your Word that prayer is the key to being set free, and prayer with fasting together is even more powerful. I pray You will help me to understand the authority You have given me in prayer to release Your power from heaven in order to see freedom happen in my life and in the lives of those for whom I pray. I know that many good things will not happen without prayer and fasting, so I ask You to help me to do both. Lead me according to Your perfect will. In Jesus' name I pray.

50

PRAYING *for* YOUR NATION

⚬⚬⌒ Read and Consider ⌒⚬⚬
Jeremiah 6:16-19

"This is what the LORD says: 'Stand at the crossroads and
look; ask for the ancient paths, ask where the good way
is, and walk in it, and you will find rest for your souls.
But you said, "We will not walk in it."...I am bringing
disaster on this people, the fruit of their schemes, because
they have not listened to my words'" (Jeremiah 6:16,19).

Notice what God said to the sinful nations: "Stand...look...ask...
walk." In other words, "Look for the right way to go and then
follow it." And the reward for doing that meets everyone's deepest
longing—"and you will find rest for your souls." Unfortunately, the
response of far too many nations to God is, "We will not walk in it."

The consequence for any nation that forsakes God and His ways is
serious. Even though you and I and millions of other believers have
not forsaken God and His ways, many others in our nation have.
But God gives us a way to respond to His warnings of judgment
by confessing the sins of our nation before Him and asking Him
to heal our land: "If my people, who are called by my name, will
humble themselves and pray and seek my face and turn from their
wicked ways, then will I hear from heaven and will forgive their sin
and will heal their land" (2 Chronicles 7:14).

He didn't say that all people in a nation must be perfect in their
heart and actions in order to receive His blessings. If that were
the case, there would never be a nation that was blessed. We can,
however, "stand in the gap" and be the one person willing to pray.
Ezekiel described the sad situation when not one person could be

found to pray: "I looked for a man among them who would build up the wall and stand before me in the gap on behalf of the land so I would not have to destroy it, but I found none" (Ezekiel 22:30).

God allows those of us who are called by His name to humble ourselves and repent for the sins of our nation so that we can continue to receive the blessings He has for us. We can stand in the gap on behalf of our unrepentant nation. Let's pray that we will be the ones who stand at the crossroads, look for the ancient paths, ask where the good way is, and walk in it. And may many others follow our example.

~∞⊃C♢♢~

Lord, I come humbly before You and confess the sins of my nation. Even though there are many people who believe in You, far too many have refused to walk Your way. I stand in the gap at the crossroads and look for the good way and pray for many more to join me in walking according to Your law so that disaster will be averted in our land. Raise up an army of intercessors who will do battle against our spiritual enemy by standing together in prayer, seeking Your presence and walking in Your ways. In Jesus' name I pray.

51

PRAYING *for* SPIRITUAL LEADERS *and* SERVANTS

Read and Consider

Acts 6:1-7

*"They presented these men to the apostles, who prayed
and laid their hands on them" (Acts 6:6).*

People in full-time ministry need our prayer support. In the case
of these men who were chosen to handle the food ministry, they
were spiritually wise men who would be taking on a huge responsibility. Their job would allow the apostles to focus on preaching
and teaching.

Every job within the body of Christ—the church—is important,
as signified by the care in which the food-program workers were
chosen in the early church. The men chosen to deal with the daily
distribution of food had to be men who were "known to be full of
the Spirit and wisdom" (6:3). When the apostles prayed for them
and laid their hands on them, it signified that they were set apart
for special service to God (Numbers 27:22-23; Deuteronomy 34:9).

Carefully choosing and praying for church workers is important
because Satan's attacks go first to those who are making a difference
for the cause of Christ. Have you ever noticed that when a church is
winning souls, attacks seem to come from all sides? Little problems
creep in, disagreements arise, temptations sprout like weeds. How
do we fight this? By praying for those who minister and serve.

Pray for the Sunday school teacher who has a class full of children.
Pray for the pastoral staff who must make decisions that affect the
entire congregation. Pray for the administrative staff who carry a

heavy load of paperwork each week. Pray for the people who volunteer their time with the youth group. Pray that each of them will be able to stand against every temptation and that none will fall into the traps of the enemy.

Spiritual leadership at all levels is serious business. Be sure to hold up these servants in prayer.

God, I ask You to bless all those in full-time ministry. I pray first of all for my pastor, that You would bless him and his family in every way. I pray for all other pastors and staff members at my church to be blessed by You and led by Your Spirit. Keep them all safe and protect them from any attacks of the enemy. Help them to stand strong against every temptation. I pray for those who care for children to be able to impart Your love to them in such a way that they are always drawn closer to You. In Jesus' name I pray.

52

PRAYING *for* HEALING

~~~ Read and Consider ~~~

Jeremiah 17:14-18

"Heal me, O LORD, and I will be healed" (Jeremiah 17:14).

Healing and body care are two different things. When you ask God to heal you, this is something *He* does. Taking care of your body is something *you* do. Both are vitally important.

God knows we are a fallen race and can't do everything perfectly. That's why He sent Jesus to be our Healer. But He also calls us to be good stewards over everything He gives us, including our body. He wants us to live in balance and temperance and to take care not to abuse our body in any way. He wants us to glorify Him in the care of our bodies because we are the temple of His Holy Spirit.

Many of us tend to think, "Everything I have is the Lord's—except for my eating habits. Those are mine." Or we think, "My life is the Lord's, but my body belongs to me, and I can do with it whatever feels good." But when we are the Lord's, our body has to be surrendered to Him just like everything else. Caring for our body is not something we can do successfully independent of God.

I've actually heard people say, "I don't worry about taking care of my body because the Lord can just heal me when I get sick." This kind of presumptuous thinking is dangerous and can get us into trouble. Satan's plan for our lives is to do the very thing that will hurt us the most. We help him along by that kind of attitude. We sabotage our lives by not doing what's best for our bodies and our health. Ask God to help you resist what is bad for you and to be disciplined enough to do what's right. God loves and values you. He

111

created you. You are where His Holy Spirit dwells. He wants you to love and value yourself enough to take good care of your body.

However, even after all of our efforts toward taking proper care of ourselves, we can still get sick. And we need Jesus, our Healer, to heal us. Don't hesitate to ask Him for His healing touch upon your body.

Dear Lord, how grateful I am that You came as our Healer. Thank You for mercifully understanding how much we need Your healing hand. I ask for Your healing touch upon my body today and whenever I need it. I know when You heal me, I will be healed completely. At the same time I ask for Your guidance and wisdom in knowing how to take care of my body—the temple of Your Holy Spirit. Give me knowledge and strength to be able to always do the right thing in that regard. In Jesus' name I pray.

53

STRUGGLING *in* PRAYER

⎯⎯ Read and Consider ⎯⎯
Genesis 32

"Jacob was left alone, and a man wrestled with him till daybreak. When the man saw that he could not overpower him, he touched the socket of Jacob's hip so that his hip was wrenched as he wrestled with the man. Then the man said, 'Let me go, for it is daybreak.' But Jacob replied, 'I will not let you go unless you bless me'" (Genesis 32:24-26).

Does prayer ever seem like a struggle to you? Often our prayer times may seem more like wrestling matches than conversations, but this passage lets us know that amazing transformations can come out of the struggles we experience in prayer.

Up until this particular encounter with God, Jacob's life had been characterized by his attempts to get ahead on his own, his deceitful plots to obtain blessings, and his manipulations to make his life work out the way he wanted it to. He had not given God control and had not trusted the Lord to carry out His plans.

However, when the stranger came along and wrestled with him, Jacob was at a point in his life when he was alone and genuinely fearful about what was going to happen to him and to his family. He was about to meet his brother again, who had every right to hate him. Jacob had no idea what his brother's plans might be. During the struggle with the stranger (who turned out to be God, 32:30), Jacob told the stranger his name—the equivalent of a confession, because his name literally meant "supplanter" or "usurper." This confession led to transformation. Jacob received the blessing from his opponent—a new name and a new future. He had been changed by the confrontation. He also received an injury that resulted in a lifetime limp—an ever-present reminder of what had happened.

If you want to experience life-changing prayer, be honest with God about who you are and confess it. For example, say, "Lord, I have been fearful," or "Lord, I have been a doubter." Then say, "Lord, help me to rise above who I am now to who You have called me to be." Despite Jacob's past, God's plans prevailed in his life, but not without a struggle. Don't be afraid to struggle in prayer, knowing that God will use any measures necessary in order to carry out His plans for your life. Like Jacob, hang on and don't give up until you get the blessing that will change you forever.

Lord, I desire to know You better so that I can experience all the blessings You have for me. I confess I don't pray as much as I would like to, and I have times of fear and doubt, but I commit this day to trust You more and to pray without ceasing—even if it feels like a struggle—because I know I will find transformation in Your presence. In times when praying seems hard to me, help me to not waver in my faith that You always hear and will answer according to Your will. In Jesus' name I pray.

54

KNOW *the* SOURCE

"He told them what Micah had done for him, and said,
'He has hired me and I am his priest.' Then they said to
him, 'Please inquire of God to learn whether our journey
will be successful.' The priest answered them, 'Go in peace.
Your journey has the LORD's approval'" (Judges 18:4-6).

Looking to other people for counsel can be a very wise thing to
do—that is, when we seek wisdom from the right sources. In
this case, however, the five warriors from the tribe of Dan looked
to a priest who inquired of "god" by using idols and other images,
not the true God of Israel. Later in the story, this priest proved to
be fickle and disloyal as he abandoned his former master in a time
of distress for a better offer. Not exactly a trustworthy source of
information!

When you are seeking God's guidance, you might want to ask
everyone you know for their opinions—thinking that the more
counselors the better. But instead of rushing to get a quick word,
stop and pray first. Ask God to give you real discernment. Test the
source before you follow any advice. Ask only those who can offer
true wisdom from the Lord.

The men from Dan had the right idea—they inquired about
God's will. But they stopped inquiring when they heard the priest's
word. We must take everything we hear and make sure that it is
consistent with God's Word. That is the most trustworthy source
and the only one we can always count on.

Lord, I turn to You for all wisdom, direction, and guidance. When I must seek advice from another person, help me to know if that person speaks from godly knowledge or not. Teach me to always test the input of others against Your Word. You are my ultimate source for all knowledge and the giver of true wisdom. Give me discernment to know when instruction is from You and when it comes from human thoughts only.
In Jesus' name I pray.

55

PRAY BEFORE YOU ACT

<small>⟨⟨⟨ Read and Consider ⟩⟩⟩</small>
1 Chronicles 14:8-17

*"Now the Philistines had come and raided the Valley
of Rephaim; so David inquired of God: 'Shall I
go and attack the Philistines? Will you hand them
over to me?' The LORD answered him, 'Go, I will
hand them over to you'"* (1 Chronicles 14:9-10).

David was finally made king of all Israel. Suddenly, he faced his
first challenge as the ruler of the land. The Philistines decided
to test his strength by invading territory under his control. The new
king could have taken this threat as a personal challenge to prove his
fitness to rule. Instead, he turned to God for wisdom in responding
to the attack. He didn't do anything before asking God for direction.
He prayed before proceeding.

Twice God instructed David to attack. His permission was
specific. So was His promise of victory. Israel would defeat the
Philistines because God would "hand them over." Interestingly, both
armies took their "gods" into battle. The true God of Israel won;
the gods of the Philistines were left lying on the battlefield like dry
wood ready for burning. "The Philistines had abandoned their gods
there, and David gave orders to burn them in the fire" (14:12).

Then the Philistines returned for round two. It's not clear exactly
why. Perhaps they needed to rescue their gods or try out some new
ones, or perhaps they thought David's first victory was just begin-
ner's luck. David prayed again and received new marching orders.
The Philistines were defeated again.

David's actions in this passage reveal several significant lessons about prayer. First, no matter how sudden or major a threat, we need to pray *before* we respond. Second, God brings the victory. Third, just because we have prayed and seen an "enemy" defeated doesn't mean we won't face that same threat again. Fourth, prayer allows us to receive direction from God that may include a different kind of action than we have taken previously.

Although we can't always see the problems we avoided because we prayed, all too often we see the bad things that happen when we act and don't pray. Ask God to help you always pray before you take any action or make any decision.

~~~

Dear Lord, I pray I will always inquire of You first before I take action. I don't want to assume that because You instructed me in a certain way before, You will instruct me in the same way each time I am faced with a similar situation. I don't want to mistakenly think I have all the answers when only You have all the answers for my life. Just as David inquired of You the direction he needed with regard to attacking the enemy, he also failed to inquire of You when the enemy set a trap for him by leading him into temptation. Keep me from the pride that can lead me astray into enemy territory.
In Jesus' name I pray.

56

FACING YOUR FEARS

⤚⤙ Read and Consider ⤚⤙
Job 3

*"What I feared has come upon me; what I dreaded
has happened to me. I have no peace, no quietness; I
have no rest, but only turmoil" (Job 3:25-26).*

Job was considered by God to be a righteous man, and yet Job had
fear. He feared something happening to his children. He feared
failing health. He feared losing everything. When each one of these
fears came true, he said, "I have no rest, but only turmoil." Overwhelmed with grief, Job wished he had never been born. He had
lived according to God's laws, had worshipped God rather than
his possessions, and still he was afflicted. Who can criticize Job for
his reaction? How many of us have lost everything—including our
children, health, and possessions? How would we respond to such
a horrible situation?

When the thing we fear most comes upon us, the only way to
react is to praise God in the midst of it. That doesn't mean we have
to act as though nothing bad has happened. Besides, healthy grief
is important. But we must still recognize the things about God that
are always true no matter what is happening and how afraid we are.

Whatever your deepest fears are right now, bring every one of
them to God. Thank Him that He is greater than any of them.
Thank Him that in His presence all fear is gone. "Blessed is the man
who fears the LORD, who finds great delight in his commands...He
will have no fear of bad news; his heart is steadfast, trusting in the
LORD" (Psalm 112:1,7).

God's love can take away your fear. His love gives the power to

119

stand against the enemy of your soul when he wants fear to overwhelm you. And even if your worst fears do come upon you, God's love assures you that He will walk with you every step of the way toward restoration.

⧼∽∽∾⚬ᴄ⚬∾∽⧽

Lord, I lift up to You my deepest fears and ask that You would deliver me from them. Set me free from all dread and anxiety about the things that frighten me. Thank You that in Your presence all fear is gone. Thank You that in the midst of Your perfect love, all trepidation in me is dissolved. I know You are greater than anything I face. Even so, I know that if what I fear comes upon me, You will lift me above it or walk me through it. Either way, I trust in You and will praise You all the way.
In Jesus' name I pray.

57

COMMIT YOUR WORK *to* GOD

*"May the favor of the Lord our God rest upon
us; establish the work of our hands for us—yes,
establish the work of our hands" (Psalm 90:17).*

What's on your "To Do" list for today? Do you have a job to get to, a home to clean, someone to care for? Do you feel sometimes as if you're constantly busy, continually on the move, and yet at the end of the day you wonder if you have accomplished all that you should have? How about your work? Do you regularly ask God to bless it?

The psalmist recognized that people "are like the new grass of the morning—though in the morning it springs up new, by evening it is dry and withered" (90:5-6). Our days, quite literally, are numbered. "The length of our days is seventy years—or eighty, if we have the strength" (90:10). This reminder of our own mortality reinforces the need to commit every task we undertake to God and to ask for His blessing upon it.

We can start by making it a habit to turn our day over to the Lord when we first wake up. Then ask for His help in all that we have to do and thank Him that He will enable us to do it. "The one who calls you is faithful and he will do it" (1 Thessalonians 5:24).

When you thank God and give Him charge over every endeavor you undertake, right down to the smallest detail of your day, He will establish the work of your hands. When you ask God to bless the work you do and to enable you to do it better and better, you will see the quality of your work improve in the way you always dreamed it would.

*Dear God, I pray You would bless my work and establish
it. I commit all of the work I do to You so that it may be
used for Your glory. Give me the strength to accomplish
what I must do each day, and the wisdom and ability
to do it well. Be in charge of every detail of my work so
that it will find favor with others and be successful. Give
me clarity of mind and the ability to always improve
in my work. Keep me from carelessness or from slacking
off so that I will always take care of the details well.
In Jesus' name I pray.*

58

How *to* Always Do God's Will

❧ Read and Consider ❧
1 Thessalonians 5:12-28
---

*"Be joyful always; pray continually; give thanks
in all circumstances, for this is God's will for you
in Christ Jesus" (1 Thessalonians 5:16-18).*

What do you do when you pray and pray about something, and God doesn't seem to answer? For example, what if you've been praying about an important decision, and now time is running out? You have to know what to do right away, but still God seems silent. What do you do then? When that happens, always do what you *know* is God's will. And it is always God's will to be joyful, to *continue* praying, and to give Him thanks regardless of your circumstances (5:16-18). Praise, prayer, and a joyful heart are vital when you need to know God's will for your life.

To "be joyful always" means we have to make a choice. We can't always choose how we feel, but we *can* choose how we respond to our feelings. We can make a decision to be joyful *in spite* of how we feel. The way we do that is to never allow our feelings or our circumstances to interfere with our worship. Whatever the situation is, when we continually acknowledge God's greatness in the midst of whatever is happening, we experience the joy of the Lord.

To "pray continually" means to pray about everything right when you think about it, allowing prayer to become a natural first response to whatever is happening. Imagine how complicated our lives would be if we had to remember to tell our heart to beat and our lungs to breathe. How much time would we spend if we had to schedule all the body repairs that go on around the clock without

123

our conscious attention? The challenge to pray continually is an invitation to develop a prayer life that simply goes on constantly in the background, like our lungs breathing and our heart beating, no matter what is happening in our life.

To "give thanks" is the main reason to pray. It's expressing gratitude for who God is and all He has done. It's deciding to be grateful even in the tough times—times of darkness, sadness, or despair. It's saying "thank you" to God in moments when we can't see the whole picture, knowing He will shed His light on the situation. We need to give thanks "in all circumstances" because something good always happens when we thank God. We become more receptive to God's will. We gain the mind of Christ and the leading of the Holy Spirit. We invite God to work in our situation. That means if we were leaning toward doing something that wasn't actually the will of God, our heart would open up to what He wants for us, and our mind would change.

So when you are waiting to know God's will for your future, do what you know is always God's will right now: Continue praying and praising and letting the joy of the Lord rise in your heart.

❧

> *God, I know it is always Your will for me to be joyful and*
> *pray often and give thanks to You in all circumstances. Help*
> *me to remember to do Your will in this regard, even when I*
> *don't see answers to my prayers as I would like. No matter*
> *what is happening in my life, I know You are greater than*
> *anything I face. There is always good reason to praise You*
> *at the beginning of my day and throughout each hour until*
> *I go to sleep at night. I choose to live every day in Your joy.*
> *In Jesus' name I pray.*

59

STOP PRAYING *and* START MOVING

∽ Read and Consider ∼
Exodus 14

"Then the LORD said to Moses, 'Why are you crying out
to me? Tell the Israelites to move on'" (Exodus 14:15).

Many passages of Scripture speak of the importance of crying out
to God in times of distress. In Lamentations we read, "Arise,
cry out in the night...pour out your heart like water in the presence
of the Lord" (Lamentations 2:19). There comes a point, however,
when the time for crying out is past and our clear instruction from
the Lord is to take action.

That's what God said to Moses. The Israelites didn't need to worry
about the details; God would take care of everything. He would help
His people by obstructing the sight of the Egyptians with clouds
and darkness. He would give the Israelites light. He would cause
the wind to dry up the sea bottom. They didn't need more desperate
prayer. They needed to get moving!

They may have been tempted to just wait. "This can't be what
God wants us to do! It's too dangerous! It's too frightening! How do
we know we'll make it? Let's just keep praying about this."

Sometimes prayer is an excuse for inaction.

Famed missionary Amy Carmichael once wrote a simple rhyme
to illustrate the importance of following through with action once
we have thoroughly prayed over a matter:

> *A centipede was happy till*
> *One day, a toad in fun*
> *Said, "Pray, which leg goes after which?"*

Which strained his mind to such a pitch
He lay distracted in a ditch,
Considering how to run.

When you hear God telling you to move in a certain direction, take two words of advice: *Do it!*

If you delay, you may well find yourself "distracted in a ditch, considering how to run." When the way is clear, remember the Lord's instruction to the Israelites through Moses—"Move on!"

Holy Father, help me to understand, as I am in prayer and waiting for a leading from You, when it is time to take action. Help me to be wise enough to recognize the answers to my prayers when they come in ways I am not expecting. Give me the knowledge of Your will that lets me know when it is time to stand up and take steps of faith. I see from Your Word that there is a time to stop praying about doing something and start doing it. Help me to always know when that is.
In Jesus' name I pray.

60

DON'T NEGLECT YOUR
WALK WITH GOD

∽ Read and Consider ∽
Haggai 1:1-11

*"'You expected much, but see, it turned out to be little. What
you brought home, I blew away. Why?' declares the LORD
Almighty. 'Because of my house, which remains a ruin,
while each of you is busy with his own house'" (Haggai 1:9).*

In Haggai's time, the people had been returned to their land after
exile in Babylon. But instead of getting down to work rebuilding
their spiritual lives by rebuilding God's temple, they were more
concerned with the condition of their own homes, more concerned
with how they looked to others than with the time they spent in
communion with God.

It is a warning to us to not be concerned with outward appearances and selfish pursuits, but rather to be concerned with the
condition of our hearts and the things that touch the heart of God.

Haggai had stern words for his people. He admonished them to
get their priorities straight! We too have to always place God first in
our lives and remember that any work we attempt for Him without
His blessing and guidance will be unproductive. Our material possessions will not satisfy us like He will.

Don't allow anything to keep you from your daily prayer time.
Do whatever it takes to be with God. Ask Him to help you not
neglect your relationship with Him. What you do in the Spirit—your
praise, worship, and prayer—lasts for eternity.

*God, help me to not be concerned with outward
appearances, selfish pursuits, and the condition of my own
house, but rather to be concerned with spiritual growth,
unselfish service, and the condition of Your house. I want
to always have my priorities in order so that my walk
with You continues to grow closer and deeper. Help me
to always put You first so that I never neglect my daily
prayer time—talking to You and worshipping You—nor
time in Your Word learning more about Your ways.
In Jesus' name I pray.*

61

ASK *for* BOLDNESS *to*
SHARE YOUR FAITH

⤚ Read and Consider ⤙
Philemon 1:4-7

*"I pray that you may be active in sharing your faith,
so that you will have a full understanding of every
good thing we have in Christ" (Philemon 1:6).*

The moment we meet Jesus for the first time, our lives are changed forever. It's a moment we never forget. Why, then, is it so hard to introduce others to Him? After all, we understand the incredible effect knowing Jesus will have on their lives for all eternity. Jesus saves us and transforms our lives, and then He gives us the wonderful privilege of being a part of someone else's salvation and transformation. But when we have an opportunity to speak to others about Him, we can be filled with trepidation. For some of us, the pressure of wanting to be sure we say the right thing causes us to hesitate. We are afraid we might say something wrong, say it insensitively, or turn someone off entirely. We fear we might be rejected and not be a good representative of Christ. That's why prayer in advance of that is crucial!

The apostle Paul's prayer is a model for us as believers and members of the family of God. Sharing our faith is a divine calling and is instrumental in furthering the work of God, but we can't do it without God's power. That's why we need to pray for God's enablement before we share our faith. We need to ask God to open up opportunities to talk about Jesus and to give us the ability to communicate His love in such a way that people can understand it and are attracted to it.

Pray often that you will be able to share your faith whenever the opportunity presents itself and that you will have the perfect words to say. Pray for God to soften the hearts of those you speak to and open their ears and eyes so that their hearts can receive the truth.

God, help me to get over any inhibitions I have about sharing my faith with unbelievers. I know of no greater gift than to give someone Your love and the good news of salvation in Christ, but I always want to be sensitive to Your leading so that I don't come off as insensitive to others. Help me to have a perfect sense of timing and the right words to say. I remember how turned off I was to the truth about You and Your Son when it was not said in a loving and caring way. I want people to see Your love in me expressed toward them in a manner that draws them to You.
In Jesus' name I pray.

62

Delivering God's Message

*"Should I not be concerned about that
great city?" (Jonah 4:11).*

God had given Jonah a second chance. "Go to the great city of Nineveh" had been the directive (1:2), and Jonah had gone the other direction. But God caught up with him, sent a fish to provide personal transportation back to shore, and said again to Jonah, "Go to the great city of Nineveh" (3:2). And this time, Jonah went.

What a compassionate God! He could have let His reluctant prophet drown in the ocean, but He didn't. He had a message for Nineveh, and He wanted Jonah to deliver it.

God always offers His grace and compassion to everyone—even those who might seem to be least deserving. Somewhere in Nineveh surely someone was seeking divine intervention, someone believed there had to be more to life, and they were looking to God for help. And God heard their prayer and sent Jonah to bring a message—with powerful results. The people's hearts were ripe to hear from God.

God hears the cries of those who seek Him. When people call out to Him on behalf of a city, He will send someone with a message. When people don't seek God, and when their hearts become hard and filled with evil desires, God will allow destruction to come upon them.

You have surely received God's compassion and seen His loving touch on your life. All around you are people who need to know God's love and compassion for them, too. Many of them may look carefree, but who knows the deep longings in their hearts and the questions they may be asking? They may be praying, "Lord, send someone to speak the truth and show me the right way to live."

Ask God to show you if perhaps He is sending you or asking you to intercede on someone's behalf.

~~~

Lord, I know there are people all around me who need
to hear Your message of hope and truth—people whom I
might not even notice, but whom You love deeply. Reveal
them to me so I can pray for them and perhaps speak
an encouraging word from You to them. Prepare their
hearts to receive from me and most of all from You.
Sometimes I don't want to pray for people who are totally
sold out to their own sin and evil ways, but I know You
have not given up on them. Help me not to give up
on them either and show me how to pray for them.
In Jesus' name I pray.

63

The POWER *of* FORGIVENESS

Read and Consider
Mark 11:20-25

"And when you stand praying, if you hold anything against anyone, forgive him, so that your Father in heaven may forgive you your sins" (Mark 11:25).

Of all the commands in Scripture, the instruction to forgive those who have hurt us is one of the most difficult to keep. Our natural human tendency is to hold on to the hurt inflicted upon us, to nurse our wounds and hold grudges. Or, at the very least, we separate ourselves forever from the individual who is the source of our pain so that we cannot be hurt by that person again.

There are times, such as in cases of abuse, when physical separation is necessary. When a crime has been committed, justice and forgiveness go hand in hand. The courts of law must hold a perpetrator accountable, and God will hold that person accountable in the final judgment, but we must still forgive that person. In these verses, Jesus was talking about the spiritual obligation that we have to forgive each other because we have been so graciously forgiven by our heavenly Father. To refuse to forgive others reveals that our hearts do not understand the level of forgiveness we have received.

To forgive does not mean we necessarily forget; we may remember, but we choose not to allow the memory to keep us bitter. We don't replay the offense over and over in our mind. To forgive does not mean to say that what happened to hurt us doesn't matter; it *does* matter or it wouldn't need forgiveness. But we must remember that forgiving someone doesn't make that person right; it makes *you* free.

When you forgive, you are set free from the bondage of carrying around the hurt, the pain, the grudge. You can let it go and move on with your life.

When we choose not to forgive, we end up stuck in the past and walking in the dark (1 John 2:9-11). Because we can't see clearly, we stumble around in confusion. This throws our judgment off and we make mistakes. We become weak, sick, and bitter. Other people notice all this because unforgiveness shows in the face, words, and actions of those who have it. People see it, even if they can't specifically identify what it is, and they don't feel comfortable around it.

The good news is that when we choose to forgive, not only do we benefit, but so do the people around us.

Lord, I pray You would reveal any place in my heart where I have not forgiven someone. I know I have asked this before, but I also know how easy it is to let resentment build up, even though I try not to allow that to happen. I don't want to inhibit the forgiveness You have for me because I have not forgiven someone else. Every time I pray, show me anyone I need to forgive, and I will do that immediately. Enable me to let go of hurts and disappointments completely. In Jesus' name I pray.

64

PRAYING *for* SOMEONE WHO DOESN'T DESERVE IT

❧ Read and Consider ❧

1 Kings 13:1-10

"Then the king said to the man of God, 'Intercede with the LORD your God and pray for me that my hand may be restored.' So the man of God interceded with the LORD, and the king's hand was restored and became as it was before" (1 Kings 13:6).

Have you ever felt God calling you to pray for someone who you thought didn't deserve it? Do you know of people who ignore or even mock God, but when disaster strikes they want God to make it better? Have you ever struggled with the temptation to say, "Why should I pray for you when you show such disrespect for God?" The prophet Ahijah had good reason to feel that way when God sent him to confront the king. But he prayed anyway.

Jeroboam led a rebellion against Solomon's son Rehoboam and became the king of the northern ten tribes of Israel. Ahijah the prophet had foretold Jeroboam's success (11:29-40). Because Jeroboam didn't control Jerusalem, he feared that people's loyalty would be undermined if they continued to travel to the temple there to worship. So he instituted his own religion, complete with golden calves and altars (12:25-33). When God's messenger, Ahijah, showed up with a prophecy against the pagan altar, the king was offended. But when he pointed toward Ahijah to have him arrested, the king's hand instantly shriveled up.

Immediately, Jeroboam asked Ahijah to "intercede with the LORD your God." Even though he needed help, Jeroboam couldn't bring himself to acknowledge God as the God he should worship; instead, this was the *prophet's* God, not his. The fact that God healed him can only be seen as God's grace extended toward a rebel. But Jeroboam missed that point because he continued to promote his own religion. But Jeroboam's persistent rejection of God led to the destruction of his entire family.

And Ahijah was willing to pray for Jeroboam immediately, in spite of the fact that Jeroboam had threatened his life. This kind of praying isn't easy. But we are commanded to do it. Ahijah was under orders to announce judgment on the false religion Jeroboam was leading, but given a chance to pray for the wayward king, he didn't hesitate. Jesus said, "Love your enemies and pray for those who persecute you" (Matthew 5:44). We must remember that God is willing to listen to prayers for *us* when we don't deserve it. And we must not hesitate to pray for *others* even when we think *they* don't deserve it.

Lord, help me to obey Your commandment to love my enemies and to pray for those who persecute me. I know You have heard and answered the prayers of others for me when I didn't deserve it; help me to do the same for them. Give me the heart of love You have so that I can pray for people who hurt or disappoint me. Help me to never withhold prayer for someone because I think they are undeserving. Enable me to do what You are calling me to do with regard to praying for others. In Jesus' name I pray.

65

FATHER, I FORGIVE THEM

<small>⤙ Read and Consider ⤚</small>
Luke 23:32-34

*"Jesus said, 'Father, forgive them, for they do not
know what they are doing.' And they divided
up his clothes by casting lots" (Luke 23:34).*

I don't know about you, but when I've just been hurt by someone, the last thing I want to do is pray for that person. Most of us are more interested in focusing on some kind of justice so that the offending person will have to pay for the hurt or damage he or she has inflicted. But not Jesus.

Jesus, who had done nothing wrong, was brutally beaten within an inch of His life. His head was pierced with a crown of long, thick thorns. His skin was slashed. His hands and feet had spikes driven through them. His cross was dropped into a hole in the ground. He hung there, naked and humiliated, for all the world to laugh at and scorn. Some said, "He saved others; let him save himself if he is the Christ of God, the Chosen One" (23:35). The way they crucified Him is horrifying beyond what we can imagine. Yet as Jesus was hanging on the cross and dying in agony, He prayed for the men who were killing Him. "Father, forgive them, for they do not know what they are doing." Such amazing forgiveness and love is hard to fathom.

As we look at the injustices in our lives, how do they compare with what Jesus endured? If He could forgive His torturers, surely we can choose to forgive too. Some of us have very deep wounds that may require time before total forgiveness is worked in us. But in most injustices that we've experienced, we can decide to let go of them quickly and completely and choose to forgive the offenders.

The good news is we can ask God to help us forgive. We can ask Him to show us His perspective in the matter. We can pray for Him to help us remember what Jesus endured and be able to say, "Father, I forgive them whether they knew what they were doing or not. I forgive them, not because they deserve it, but because I want to be like You."

Lord, I pray You would help me to forgive others the way You do. You willingly forgive the worst of sins when people are repentant. Help me take my focus off whether people deserve to be forgiven or not, and instead focus on becoming more like You. It is only with Your enablement that I can forgive the seemingly unforgivable things people do. Help me forgive them completely because I want to do what pleases You. In Jesus' name I pray.

66

WHY WE DO WHAT WE DO

Leviticus 10:1-7

*"Aaron's sons Nadab and Abihu took their censers, put fire
in them and added incense; and they offered unauthorized
fire before the LORD, contrary to his command. So fire
came out from the presence of the LORD and consumed
them, and they died before the LORD" (Leviticus 10:1-2).*

Things you do over and over can become very routine. For example, if you perform a ritual enough times, even a sacred one, you can easily forget to honor the full significance of it. What's surprising, however, is to find that even when these Old Testament spiritual rituals were relatively new, some worshippers still struggled to keep the significance of their actions fresh in their minds. Nadab and Abihu were prime examples. They took lightly something that should have been holy, and they paid the ultimate price for their mistake.

From the description given to us at the opening of Leviticus 10, we know that Nadab and Abihu had disregarded instructions they'd been given. This disregard was not simply a mistake—it was an act of disrespect toward God, who had given the instructions. Their disregard seems completely out of place when you consider who these brothers were—the sons of Aaron, the nephews of Moses. They had seen miracles, walked across dry land in the middle of the Red Sea, and eaten manna. They were first-generation eyewitnesses. Their father had become the first high priest of the Israelite nation, and they, as his sons, had been welcomed into the priesthood. Exodus 24:9-10 even tells us that Nadab and Abihu were among 74 men who had climbed the mountain with Moses and had actually *seen* God.

Yet, when the time came to honor God with obedience, they just didn't think it was important enough to do what God wanted.

Have you ever become lax in that way? Do you pray as often as God wants you to? Are you spending time daily in His Word? Are those two spiritual disciplines as fresh and alive as they should be? If not, ask God to give you new excitement about spending time with Him. Ask Him to take away any apathy or carelessness on your part. Do whatever it takes to keep yourself from just going through the motions. Reconnect to the passion and meaning of being in God's presence.

⌒⌒∽⊃⊂⌒⌒

Holy Father, help me to never be careless about Your ways or Your Word. Enable me to not allow anything that has to do with my worship of You to become lifeless or like a ritual that has lost its depth of meaning. Keep the expressions of prayer, praise, and reading in Your Word fresh and alive in my heart so that I will always have a passionate hunger for Your presence. I see in Your Word how not doing things Your way brings death into our lives. Keep me always sensitive to Your will for me.
In Jesus' name I pray.

67

ACKNOWLEDGE GOD *in* EVERY AREA *of* YOUR LIFE

⟊ Read and Consider ⟊
Proverbs 3:1-18

"Trust in the LORD with all your heart and lean not on your own understanding; in all your ways acknowledge him, and he will make your paths straight" (Proverbs 3:5-6).

We have to trust that God's ways are always right and not try to figure things out on our own or make up our own rules. And we have to acknowledge God in every area of our lives.

We must acknowledge Him first of all as Jesus our Savior, as our heavenly Father, and as the Holy Spirit our Comforter. Then we have to acknowledge Him as the One who meets all of our needs and is Lord over every area of our lives. That means we acknowledge Him as Lord over our relationships, our work, our activities, our finances, our homes, our bodies, and our marriages.

Is there any place in your life that you have not turned completely over to God? If so, say, "Lord, I invite You to be Lord over this area of my life." If you are not sure, ask God to show you. He will. And when you see some area where you have not fully acknowledged God as Lord, pray, "Lord, I acknowledge You in this area of my life, and I ask You to reign there. I want to recognize You in everything I do so that I can honor and serve You. Thank You that You will direct my steps and make my paths straight." We must not depend on our own understanding. We must, instead, come to the Lord for guidance and wisdom so we can stay on the right path.

Heavenly Father, I ask that You would help me to trust You and Your ways and not depend on my own limited understanding of things. Help me to acknowledge You in every area of my life. If I have shut You out of any part of my life, I ask that You would reveal this to me so I can invite You to reign there. Remind me to acknowledge You in everything I do and say so that I never go off on my own way. Keep me on the straight path You have for me. In Jesus' name I pray.

68

SEEING *in the* DARK

*"The Lord told him, 'Go to the house of Judas on
Straight Street and ask for a man from Tarsus
named Saul, for he is praying'" (Acts 9:11).*

Saul had probably grown up doing a lot of praying. He was, after all, a Pharisee. He was a well-educated Jew who felt that the Christian movement was heretical and so decided to persecute the Christians ruthlessly. But on that road to Damascus, a brilliant light caused him to stop in his tracks. Jesus spoke directly to Saul and blinded him. As a result, Saul was led into the city of Damascus where he fasted and prayed as he had never done before.

Why was Saul blinded? It's difficult to do much when you are suddenly without sight. Saul didn't know if this was a permanent condition—at least until God spoke to him in a vision that Ananias would come and restore his sight.

In a terrifying instant, Jesus had made Himself and His holiness evident to Saul. During those three days that Saul fasted and prayed, he surely turned his sight inward and examined his life. He believed he had been doing the right thing by persecuting and arresting Christians, but now he knew he had been persecuting Jesus. Even as Paul prayed, God spoke to Ananias to go to him and pray for him to receive his sight and be filled with the Holy Spirit.

Often God will allow us to get to a dark place in our lives where we can't see without His help. And He often does that just before the greatest revelation to us of our purpose and calling.

Lord, just as You appeared to Saul and blinded him in order to get his attention and do a miraculous turnaround in his life, I know You have sometimes allowed me to get to a dark place in my own life where I cannot see without Your help. At those times, help me to do as Saul did and pray fervently, so that my spiritual sight can be restored and Your will be done. Whenever I come into a dark place or situation in my life, help me to trust that when I turn to You, Your light will lead me to where I should be. In Jesus' name I pray.

69

LEARNING *to* BELIEVE

"If you believe, you will receive whatever you ask for in prayer" (Matthew 21:22).

What a great promise from our Lord! All we have to do is believe. But that's not so easy, is it? It's easier to doubt than it is to have faith to believe for the answers to our prayers. But faith is not about trusting in faith itself, it's about trusting God and what He says in His Word. It's about confidently claiming the promises of God, believing that God means what He says.

Jesus promised His disciples, "You'll receive whatever you ask for in prayer," on one condition: "If you believe." Believe in what? In our own request? Does this mean we can get whatever we ask for, anything at all, no matter how grandiose our desires? The answer is no. Are we to believe in our own great faith? We would be foolish to do that. We are to believe God and trust in His perfect will.

It's important to remember that God's will never contradicts His Word. Yes, we are to pray for whatever we need, but if those needs and desires run contrary to the will of God, He is not going to give them to us. Our loving Father will not go against His own nature or give us that which is detrimental to the best that He has for us. At times, something may seem to us to be perfectly within God's will—and we should pray with all our heart—but we should still remember that only God sees the big picture. In the long run, what we are praying for may not be what's best at all.

Praying is not telling God what to do. Praying is communicating the desires of your heart. It's trusting that *God* knows what to do and He will answer in His way and in His time. Faith is believing God hears and will do the right thing. When you also pray that His will be done in your life, you can release your requests into God's hands, believing He has heard you and will do what's best.

Faith has to do with believing that God is who He says He is and will do what He says He will. In order to increase your faith, read God's Word and ask Him to help you learn to believe Him. Ask Him to give you a greater measure of faith and the ability to walk confidently in the faith He has given you.

Dear God, increase my faith to believe for great things. Help me to have faith enough to not pray too small. I know it is not about trusting in faith itself, but trusting in You. It's not about believing in my own ability to believe, but rather it is believing in Your ability and promise to hear and answer. Take away all unbelief in me. Whenever I pray, help me to trust completely that You hear me and will answer in Your way and time. In Jesus' name I pray.

70

WHEN OUR PRAYERS
DISPLEASE GOD

⸰⸱⸰ Read and Consider ⸰⸱⸰

Proverbs 28:9

*"If anyone turns a deaf ear to the law, even his
prayers are detestable" (Proverbs 28:9).*

Can it be that there is a time when our prayers actually *displease* God?

Scripture tells us that a consequence of disobedience is that our prayers will not be heard. In fact, the word "detestable" means something that is revolting, abominable, or loathsome. None of us wants God to see our prayers that way!

In order to grow in the Lord, it's important to keep asking God to show us what He wants us to do. If we don't ask, we won't know. Even when we think we are doing everything right, it's always good to pray, "Lord, show me any place in my life where I am not obeying You. I want to live by Your rules."

One of the consequences for disobedience is not getting your prayers answered. You cannot receive all God has for you if you are not living in obedience. Jesus said, "If you want to enter life, obey the commandments" (Matthew 19:17). He knew that nothing would give people more peace and confidence than knowing they are doing what God wants them to do. God's Word promises that by being obedient to His ways you will find mercy (Psalm 28:6), peace (Psalm 37:37), and blessing (Proverbs 29:18). *Not* living in obedience brings harsh consequences (15:10), unanswered prayers (28:9), and the inability to enter into the great things God has for us (1 Corinthians 6:9).

Walking in obedience has to do not only with keeping God's commandments but also with heeding God's *specific* instructions. For example, if God has instructed you to rest and you don't do it, that's disobedience. If He has told you to stop doing a certain type of work and you keep doing it, that's disobedience. If He has told you to move to another place and you don't move, that's disobedience too. Or God may ask you to take a different job, stop a certain activity, join a certain church, or change the way you've always done something. Whatever He asks you to do, remember He does this for your greatest good.

God's ways are always better than ours, and obedience to His Word clears the path for our prayers to be heard.

～∞⊃⊂ᙅᵒᵒ～

Almighty God, help me to know Your laws. Teach me Your Word so that I understand it better every time I read it. Give me insight into Your ways so that they become part of me. Speak to my heart if my thoughts, words, or actions start getting off the mark. Keep me on the right path so that my prayers are never detestable to You. Your Word says You will not hear the prayers of one who lives in disobedience to You and Your ways. Help me to always stay right with You so my prayers are acceptable in Your sight. In Jesus' name I pray.

71

ROADBLOCKS *to* PRAYER

"The LORD said to Joshua, 'Stand up! What
are you doing down on your face? Israel has
sinned; they have violated my covenant, which I
commanded them to keep'" (Joshua 7:10-11).

At least Joshua had come to the right place. In despair over the nation's recent defeat by the little city of Ai, Joshua and the nation's elders performed the proper rituals of repentance and remained there till evening. But the Lord was not impressed with their weeping and wailing. "Stand up!" God commanded. The problem was sin, and once the sinner was found out and the sin removed from the camp, the problem would be solved. God didn't need Joshua on his face at that moment; He needed Joshua to rout out the sin so the nation could move forward.

When you pray, you've come to the right place. But that's just the beginning. As part of your conversation with God, you will "hear" His words speaking to your heart. He will reveal sins to confess, actions to take, changes to make. As you read His Word, He'll make you aware of what He wants you to do. While it's good to keep reading, keep praying, and keep seeking—we still have to take action, especially where sin is concerned. When God reveals sin to you, "stand up," confess it, and take immediate steps to make any necessary changes. After all, you've got more battles ahead, and you need to be ready.

Lord, I know my prayers have no effect if I have sin in my life for which I have not repented or confessed. Reveal to me any sin I am harboring, and I will confess it so that nothing comes between You and me. I don't want to give place to any hindrances to my prayers, and I don't want to put up a roadblock to all You want to do in my life. When You reveal sin in me, help me to stand up and recognize that it is rooted in my actions and thoughts. In Jesus' name I pray.

72

BEING HONEST BEFORE GOD

∽ Read and Consider ∽

Jeremiah 12:1-13

"You are always righteous, O LORD, when I bring a case before you. Yet I would speak with you about your justice: Why does the way of the wicked prosper? Why do all the faithless live at ease?" (Jeremiah 12:1).

One remarkable thing about Jeremiah was he never hesitated to tell God what was on his mind. He didn't edit his prayers. He trusted God enough to be completely honest. God listened and responded with mercy. In this particular case, Jeremiah came to God with a compliment and two complaints. He recognized God's faithfulness—"You are always righteous" (12:1). Then Jeremiah began to pour out a list of issues he felt God needed to resolve. Among these were the prosperity and peaceful living of wicked people, which greatly irritated the prophet. Why did God allow such people to succeed?

God's response presents a beautiful picture of His patience. He gently told Jeremiah that he was out of his league in attempting to give God direction. He didn't rebuke Jeremiah; He simply told him that what he observed was a small part of a much larger picture.

God wants us to be honest with Him. He lets us bare our souls and share our hearts. Like a loving parent, He listens and is not angry or impatient. So if you have concerns and questions, bring them before your heavenly Father and lay them all at His feet. Often He will help you to see things from His perspective. God already knows what is in your heart. He wants you to be completely honest with Him about it.

*God, I know You are always good and just, and I don't
question Your ways, but I confess that sometimes I wonder
why certain people seem to get away with murder while
others, who are Your servants—and seem to have done
nothing wrong—have so much suffering in their lives. Help
me to see these things from Your perspective so that I might
help others do the same. I know that You are patient to wait
for others to repent, which means You are also patient with
me when I am slow to see the areas in me where I need to
be repentant. Help me to recognize Your mercy toward me.
In Jesus' name I pray.*

73

MAKING SACRIFICES

∞∽ Read and Consider ∼∞

Genesis 22:1-19

"Some time later God tested Abraham. He said to
him, 'Abraham!' 'Here I am,' he replied. Then God
said, 'Take your son, your only son, Isaac, whom you
love, and go to the region of Moriah. Sacrifice him
there as a burnt offering on one of the mountains I
will tell you about.' Early the next morning Abraham
got up and saddled his donkey" (Genesis 22:1-3).

Sometimes God asks the strangest things. Noah had to build an ark miles away from any body of water and put in stalls that would somehow be filled with animals. (Surely he wondered how he was going to round up the lions and keep them away from the zebras!)

But nothing quite matches the task given to Abraham. Not only did God ask him to kill his son, God was taking away from Abraham that answer to the promise he had waited 25 years to receive. Isaac was Abraham's heir, the child promised to Abraham and Sarah, the child born in their old age. For Isaac to die would also kill the dream.

Or would it?

It seems that Abraham didn't waste time worrying about it. He got up early the next morning, saddled his donkey, roused the sleepy boy and two servants, cut some wood (he would need kindling to start the fire), and set out for the three-day journey. What went through his mind during those three long days? I imagine that Abraham talked to God *a lot*. And such was Abraham's relationship with God that he trusted God. He didn't understand; he knew that obeying God would hurt him to the core, but he kept right on walking. He kept right on obeying. When he got to the place, he built an altar, bound his son, laid him on the altar, and raised the knife.

Could any of us trust God that much?

Our hearts wince at the thought of sacrificing a human being. But we would be wise to consider how this story gives an astounding picture of what God Himself would one day do for us. As Isaac carried the wood for the burnt offering, so Jesus carried His own cross to Golgotha. As Abraham placed Isaac on the altar, so God placed His Son on the cross. As Abraham raised his knife in order to kill his son in obedience to God, so God allowed Jesus to be put to death so that sin could be punished and forgiveness could be given. Abraham knew that God would provide the lamb for the offering (22:8). Many centuries later, He did. John the Baptist pointed this out to his followers: "Look, the Lamb of God, who takes away the sin of the world!" (John 1:29). How much do you trust God? Enough to die for Him?

How about enough to let a dream in your life die?

∞∽っⲥℴⲟℴ

Lord, I know You always ask me to surrender everything to You—including the dream in my heart. And even when that dream is from You, You still ask me to let go of my hold on it. So I surrender every dream I have to You right now. I don't want to cling to something You will not bless, or give up on something that is Your will for my life. I want to do what You want me to do—not just what I want to do. Help me to trust You with the desire of my heart. In Jesus' name I pray.

74

PRAYING *from a* RIGHT HEART

Psalm 66

"If I had cherished sin in my heart, the Lord would not have listened; but God has surely listened and heard my voice in prayer. Praise be to God, who has not rejected my prayer or withheld his love from me!" (Psalm 66:18-20).

The good thing about prayer—or the problem with prayer, depending on our perspective—is that we have to go to God to do it. This means we can't get away with anything. It means that any negative thoughts, bad attitudes, hardness of heart, or selfish motives are going to be revealed by the Lord. Fervent and honest prayer causes the depths of our hearts to be exposed. That can be uncomfortable. Even downright miserable. The verses above make it crystal clear that if we have any unforgiveness, bitterness, selfishness, pride, anger, irritation, or resentment in our hearts, our prayers will not be answered. Our hearts have to be right when we pray.

In the same way, God wants us to be right with others before we take our concerns or even our acts of service—our "gifts"—to Him. In what is called The Sermon on the Mount, Jesus explicitly instructed His followers on the importance of setting things right: "Therefore, if you are offering your gift at the altar and there remember that your brother has something against you, leave your gift there in front of the altar. First go and be reconciled to your brother; then come and offer your gift" (Matthew 5:23-24).

All of us jeopardize our own prayers when we don't pray them from a right heart. What is in our hearts when we pray has more effect on whether our prayers are answered than the actual prayer itself. That's why, when we come before God to pray, He asks us to first confess anything in our hearts that shouldn't be there. He does that so nothing will separate us from Him.

If you ever feel as if your prayers are not being heard, examine your heart and ask God to clearly reveal anything that you might need to confess before Him. Then that joy David felt will be your joy as well.

～～～～～

Lord, I don't want to entertain sin in my heart. I want my heart to be right before You so that You will always hear my prayers. I know I don't do everything perfectly, so I ask that by the power of Your Holy Spirit You will enable me to keep my heart pure and my hands clean. Your Word tells me that You never withhold love from me or reject my prayers, but You do wait to see if I allow sin to exist in my heart. Thank You for loving me enough to help me do what is right in Your sight. In Jesus' name I pray.

75

Pray *to* Resist Temptation

Psalm 51

*"Create in me a pure heart, O God, and renew a
steadfast spirit within me. Do not cast me from your
presence or take your Holy Spirit from me. Restore
to me the joy of your salvation and grant me a
willing spirit, to sustain me" (Psalm 51:10-12).*

D avid wrote the words of this psalm after the prophet Nathan
confronted him following David's adultery with Bathsheba.
To his credit, David recognized his own sin, and this psalm is both
a passionate plea for purity and a prayer in which David is crying
out to God to be restored into the joy of right relationship. However,
David could have spared himself much grief and sorrow (as well
as for Bathsheba and her husband) if he had taken his feelings for
Bathsheba to God in the first place.

God wants us to live in stark contrast to the world. The world is
absorbed totally in the flesh. Sexual temptation of one sort or another
is everywhere. The attitude toward casual sex and immorality in
our society has gone far beyond what most people imagined it ever
could. Those who have any sense of their own purpose and who
God created them to be know that they cannot compromise in this
area. The price is way too high. The consequences are far too great.

There is a way to resist all temptation of the flesh—especially
sexual temptation—and that is to worship God. But it must be our
first reaction, and not after the fact.

King David *should* have done this. Instead, when Bathsheba

discovered she was pregnant, David tried to cover up the adultery by arranging to have her husband killed in battle.

This all began as one sinful thought. No one ends up in adultery without thinking about it first. It's at the *first thought* that prayer should arise. David was later confronted by the prophet Nathan about what he had done, and to his credit David confessed everything and was deeply repentant. Even so, there were stiff consequences for his actions, not the least of which was the death of David and Bathsheba's baby boy. And from that time on murder, death, and treachery became a part of his family and his reign.

Everyone makes mistakes. Don't let guilt over them separate you from God or make you feel distant from Him. That is the enemy's plan to keep you from all God has for you. The way to have victory over temptation is to go immediately before the Lord when temptation first crosses your mind. Don't wait the way David did. Don't entertain it for even a moment. Go to God right away and confess it. Then praise Him as the God who is more powerful than anything that tempts you.

✧✦✧

> *God, I pray You would create in me a clean and right heart before You at all times. Help me to come to You immediately at the very first sign of temptation so that I can stop any wrong thoughts from turning into sinful actions. I don't want to ever be separated from the presence of Your Holy Spirit. Help me to resist the plan of the enemy to keep me from all You have for me. Enable me to be victorious over temptation by coming to You the moment a sinful thought crosses my mind. In Jesus' name I pray.*

76

The BLESSING *of* CONFESSING

⋘ Read and Consider ⋙
Psalm 32

"Then I acknowledged my sin to you and did not cover up
my iniquity. I said, 'I will confess my transgressions to the
LORD'—and you forgave the guilt of my sin" (Psalm 32:5).

S in always brings separation. When we behave badly toward our
family members or use our tongues carelessly so that others are
wounded, our sinful actions lead to barriers being built between
ourselves and other people.

Sin separates us from God as well. When we break any of the
commandments that He lovingly set forth for our own protection,
we put up a wall between ourselves and the One who made us. It's
a wall of our own construction. But God's Word provides a solution
to this barrier. It's called confession.

Confession has been defined as "agreeing with God about our sin."
The most common Old Testament words for sin are "transgressions"
and "iniquity," and Psalm 32 contains frequent references to these
actions that serve to separate us from God.

When we don't confess our sins, we end up trying to hide ourselves from God. Just like Adam and Eve in the garden, we feel
we can't face Him. But the problem with attempting to hide from
God is that it's impossible. The Bible says that everything we do will
be made known—even the things we said and thought in secret.
"Nothing in all creation is hidden from God's sight. Everything is
uncovered and laid bare before the eyes of him to whom we must
give account" (Hebrews 4:13).

What a frightening thought! If each of us will have to give an account, the quicker we get it straight with God—the better. In fact, the sooner we deal with the sins we *can* see, the sooner God can reveal to us the ones we *can't*. And only God knows how much of that is residing in each of us. Sin always has consequences. King David described it best when he wrote of his own unconfessed sin: "When I kept silent, my bones wasted away through my groaning all day long. For day and night your hand was heavy upon me; my strength was sapped as in the heat of summer" (Psalm 32:3-4).

Confession has a "consequence" too—a good consequence! A free and happy heart! When we confess our sins to God, we are blessed. To be blessed means to enjoy the favor of God. There is no greater blessing than knowing that your sins have been forgiven by God.

Dear Lord, I don't want anything to separate me from You and all You have for me—especially not my own unconfessed sin. I don't want to build a wall between You and me by failing to acknowledge anything I thought, said, or did that was not pleasing in Your sight. If I am too blind to see the truth about myself, reveal it to me so that I can confess it before You. I don't want to try and cover up my sin. I want to confess it before You and be forgiven and released. In Jesus' name I pray.

77

Finding Hope *in the* Midst *of* Sorrow

*"Arise, cry out in the night, as the watches of the night
begin; pour out your heart like water in the presence of the
Lord. Lift up your hands to him" (Lamentations 2:19).*

When Jeremiah wrote Lamentations, the echo of Jerusalem's crumbling walls were possibly still ringing in his ears. The cries of despair and weeping over those who had died could yet be heard. All that was left for the Israelites was the grim prospect of a bleak future.

Jeremiah, known as the "weeping prophet," responded with a grief-filled lament over the city and over the people. Like much of Jeremiah's prayer life, these verses are filled with raw emotion. They include deep reverence, anger, worship, confidence, despair, questions, and answers. All aspects of grief find expression in this brief book. Here we see how deeply the human heart can break. There's no joyful worship here, only agony.

If you ever feel such sorrow, do as Jeremiah says and "pour out your heart like water in the presence of the Lord." In your toughest hour, God invites you to hold nothing back, not even your raw emotions. In God's loving presence you will find hope.

Jeremiah finds hope in the midst of his affliction, but the promises God made to Jeremiah are for you as well. As you pour out your pain to God, as you are surrounded with bitterness and hardship (3:5), as you call out for help and it feels as if He has shut out your prayers (3:8), as your heart is pierced (3:13), as you are deprived of peace and prosperity (3:17), remember these words of Jeremiah: "Yet this I call to mind and therefore I have hope: Because of the LORD's great love we are not consumed, for his compassions never fail. They are new every morning; great is your faithfulness. I say to myself, 'The LORD is my portion; therefore I will wait for him.' The LORD is good to those whose hope is in him, to the one who seeks him; it is good to wait quietly for the salvation of the LORD" (3:21-26).

There is hope to be found in the midst of your pain. The darkness, the heartbreak, the sorrow, and the grief are not permanent. The Lord's compassion never fails. He is good to those who hope in Him, who seek Him, who wait quietly for Him.

⁓ ∞つC⊶∞ ⁓

> *Lord, I pour out my heart before You regarding things*
> *in my life that cause me grief. I lift up my hands to You*
> *because I know You are my hope and Your compassion for*
> *me never fails. Heal me of all emotional pain, and use*
> *the sorrow I have suffered for good. Enable me to pour*
> *out my heart like water—as Your Word describes—and*
> *lift my hands to You in fervent and humble prayer. I*
> *pray that in Your presence I will find total restoration.*
> *In Jesus' name I pray.*

78

Undeserved Answers *to* Prayer

"Then Jehoahaz sought the Lord's favor, and the Lord
listened to him, for he saw how severely the king
of Aram was oppressing Israel. The Lord provided
a deliverer for Israel, and they escaped from the
power of Aram. So the Israelites lived in their own
homes as they had before" (2 Kings 13:4-5).

Jehoahaz was not known for his wisdom and virtue. He was such an evil king that God sent the oppressive team of King Hazael and Prince Ben-Hadad of Aram as Jehoahaz's judgment. It seemed he was finally getting what he deserved.

But then Jehoahaz did an unexpected thing. When the oppression became too great, he did what any of us would do when our backs are against the wall and our best efforts are not enough—he prayed. An evil man was desperate and turned to God. He asked for God's help, and God gave it. That's what God does. He answers the prayers of people *who don't deserve it.*

How easy it is to believe that our answered prayers have something to do with our being good enough. Or we think that if God *hasn't* answered our prayer yet, it must be because we *aren't* good enough. Or worse, we don't pray because we think we can't impress God enough with our goodness to make Him want to answer. We forget that our best goodness still would not *deserve* God's favor.

Jehoahaz's prayer has a lot to teach us. He called out to God, knowing full well that he had given God no good reason to answer. He received God's favor, not because of who he was, but because of who God is—a gracious and compassionate God who listens to honest, humble prayers. Don't forget that God always listens whenever you pray.

〜◦◦〜ᴄᴄᴏᴏ〜

Dear Lord, I thank You that You listen to my prayers and that You answer, not according to my own goodness, but according to Yours. Help me to not let anything discourage me from coming to You in prayer—especially not my own sense that I am undeserving of Your attention and blessing. I come entirely because You are full of grace and mercy. Thank You that You have provided a deliverer for me, just as You did for Israel. Jesus, You are my Savior, Deliverer, Healer, and Provider. Thank You, Lord, that because You love me and are merciful and good, You answer my prayers, even though I do not deserve it.
In Your name I pray.

79

The IMPORTANCE *of* RESTITUTION

*"When a man or woman wrongs another in any way and
so is unfaithful to the LORD, that person is guilty and
must confess the sin he has committed. He must make
full restitution for his wrong, add one fifth to it and give
it all to the person he has wronged" (Numbers 5:6-7).*

Most of us have experienced the pain of being wronged at some
point in life. We may have had personal possessions damaged
or stolen. Worse yet, we may have lost someone we loved due to
the carelessness or callousness of another individual. There is often
no adequate compensation for the pain we suffer, but this passage
speaks of God's provision of the concept of restitution as part of
His law for the people of Israel. "To make restitution" means to
provide compensation or remuneration for the losses someone has
experienced due to the actions of another. This passage makes it clear
that to simply say "I'm sorry; please forgive me" was not sufficient.
Instead, God put into place the stipulation that the guilty party not
only had to restore what had been taken but also pay an additional
interest penalty as well. Confession included restitution.

We need to accept the fact that justice is not always served in
our imperfect world. For example, many crimes are committed for
which adequate compensation is impossible. It is usually not within
our power to demand and receive remuneration for harm done at
the hands of another. However, one avenue of justice is open to all:
a heavenly Father who sees each wrongful act committed here on
earth. In the life to come we will experience perfect justice, and in

the words of Isaiah, "Every valley shall be raised up, every mountain and hill made low; the rough ground shall become level, the rugged places a plain" (Isaiah 40:4).

Until that day comes, we need to be sure that we have not intentionally wronged another. Ask the Lord if you need to apologize and make restitution for anything in your past. The joy and freedom that come from having a clean conscience will lead you to a new level of intimacy with God. Don't put it off; take that first step today.

God, I pray You would show me if I have hurt anyone in any way. If I have, show me how I can make it up to them so that things are right between us. Help me to apologize and to ask for that person's forgiveness. I want to always have a clear conscience so that nothing will undermine the closeness I have with You. Show me how to make restitution where it is needed, and to go beyond what is expected to bring healing and forgiveness.
In Jesus' name I pray.

80

AN UNDIVIDED HEART

2 Kings 17:24-33

*"They worshiped the LORD, but they also appointed
all sorts of their own people to officiate for them as
priests in the shrines at the high places. They worshiped
the LORD, but they also served their own gods in
accordance with the customs of the nations from
which they had been brought" (2 Kings 17:32-33).*

If Samaria was anything, it was a house divided. Starting with King Jeroboam, this northern kingdom had allowed the worship of foreign gods—forgetting their spiritual roots. A succession of evil kings spiraled the nation deeper and deeper into sin, until God finally allowed it to be taken into exile by the Assyrians. The people of the northern kingdom were taken captive; then the king of Assyria brought other people from foreign lands and resettled them in Samaria. After some concerns about "what the god of that country requires" (17:26), the king sent a few exiled priests back to teach the resettled foreigners about the god of that land. The result was that people tried to combine the worship of Jehovah God with that of all the various false gods—including those whose worship practices were in direct violation of God's laws. That was a combination that was sure to bring serious consequences. When it comes to serving God, our loyalty to Him cannot be divided.

Centuries later, Jesus talked about a house divided. He had been accused of casting out demons by the power of Satan (a ludicrous accusation made by jealous people). Jesus pointed out to these accusers that He wouldn't be working against Satan by the power of Satan. A house divided is a house that will fall (see Matthew 12:24-29). And that's what happened to Samaria, not that the nation immediately disappeared, but that it never regained spiritual or political power.

Samaria is a good lesson for us. In the rush of our lives, it's easy to be divided—in our time, our energies, our focus. Without realizing it, we can be a lot like the Samaritans, serving God along with our other allegiances.

That's why prayer is so important. It unites your heart with God's. And it connects you to *who* matters more than anything else in your life. Prayer keeps your heart undivided.

***

Dear God, I pray You would keep me from ever having a divided heart. I don't want to weaken my allegiance to You by showing any allegiance to the false gods of this world. Help me to stay in close touch with You through constant and fervent prayer. Unite my heart with Yours so that it never strays. Help me to separate myself from anything that separates me from You. Help me to never live in a house divided—serving You along with false gods. Enable me to uproot and cast out every idol that has crept in.
In Jesus' name I pray.

81

Praying Without Excuses

Jeremiah 1:1-10

*"But the L*ORD *said to me, 'Do not say, "I am only a child." You must go to everyone I send you to and say whatever I command you.'...Then the L*ORD *reached out his hand and touched my mouth and said to me, 'Now, I have put my words in your mouth'"(Jeremiah 1:7,9).*

There was Jeremiah, simply minding his own business, when "the word of the LORD came" (1:2). And not just any word, but a word of divine appointment. God was giving him a whole new job description: to speak for Him to the nations. Feeling completely inadequate, Jeremiah humbly declined. After all, he couldn't speak well, and besides, he was just a kid. But God completely rejected Jeremiah's excuses.

The Lord immediately dismissed Jeremiah's concern about his youthfulness, but He did respond to Jeremiah's fear about speaking in a very specific way. The prophet described it like this: "The LORD reached out his hand and touched my mouth" (1:9). How wonderful and comforting that touch must have been. Jeremiah knew he did not need to worry any longer.

When we think up excuses for not doing God's will, what we are really saying is that we understand things better than God does. We are also saying that we think it's up to us and our abilities, rather than up to God's power and enablement. Feeling inadequate is good when it drives us to depend on God. But it's not good when that insecurity and fear cause us to say no to what God wants.

When it comes to prayer, we often have excuses for why we

can't. We may see someone who needs prayer and yet we don't step out and do it. We may think, "My prayers aren't powerful enough." "God can't use me, I'm not eloquent." "I haven't walked with God long enough."

But we must remember how God told Jeremiah that He had put words in his mouth. The Lord will do that for us when we ask Him to help us pray.

God has given us the most powerful tool in the universe: *prayer*. The power of prayer is unlimited because it's God's power, not ours. If our words release God's power to change people's hearts, bring down spiritual strongholds, or build up nations, then we are participating in the most potent force in the universe.

When you pray, start by saying, "Lord, please touch my mind and mouth and give me Your words to pray." And then pray as the Lord leads. Of course, it's only in heaven that you will be able to see all the miracles that have been brought about by your prayers. But even on earth you will one day say, "I prayed about that situation, and look what God did!"

∽∾∿∾∽

Father God, I don't want to make excuses for not doing Your will, but I feel inadequate to do the things You are calling me to do—especially in prayer. Yet I don't want fear to keep me from doing it. I want to depend on You to do it through me. I pray You would put Your words in my mouth so that I can intercede for others by the power of Your Spirit. Help me to remember that it is not my abilities that will cause me to pray in power, but it is Your Spirit in me that enables me to pray as I ought. In Jesus' name I pray.

82

FINDING ORDER *and* PEACE

~~~ Read and Consider ~~~
1 Corinthians 14:26-40

*"For God is not a God of disorder but of
peace" (1 Corinthians 14:33).*

God is not a God of disorder; He is a God of peace. Just as our households function better when there is some kind of order—you can find what you are looking for and things just make sense—our minds and hearts function better when there is a peaceful order to what we allow to influence us. We have to be careful what TV shows, magazines, and books we look at and what music, radio programs, or CDs we listen to. Those things should fill our minds with godly thoughts and feed our spirits so we are enriched, clear-minded, and peaceful. If, instead, they deplete us and leave us feeling empty, confused, anxious, and fearful, then we must turn them off and get them out of our lives.

You have a choice about what you will accept into your mind and what you won't. You can choose to take every thought captive and let Christ's mind be in you (2 Corinthians 10:5; Philippians 2:5), or you can allow the devil to feed you lies and manipulate your life. Every sin begins as a thought in the mind (Mark 7:21-22), so if you don't take control of your mind, the devil will. That's why you must be diligent to monitor what you allow into your mind.

It's up to us to fill our minds with God's Word and the words of people in whom God's Spirit resides. It's up to us to fill our hearts and thoughts with praise so that we leave no room for the enemy's propaganda. It's up to us to find order by asking the God of peace to rule our lives. Only then will we know the peace that passes all understanding.

Heavenly Father, I know You are a God of order, and order brings peace. Help me to maintain that same order and peace in my life. Give me the wisdom to not allow anything that would disturb that order and peace to influence my life. Help me to fill my mind with Your Word and my soul with Your Spirit so that there is no room for the enemy's propaganda. Enable me to recognize the source of any confusion or unrest, and resist that in prayer. Help me to take whatever action I am led by You to take.
In Jesus' name I pray.

83

The POWER of ONE

∽ Read and Consider ∼

Esther 4

*"Go, gather together all the Jews who are in Susa, and
fast for me. Do not eat or drink for three days, night
or day. I and my maids will fast as you do. When this
is done, I will go to the king, even though it is against
the law. And if I perish, I perish" (Esther 4:16).*

Have you ever thought, "I'm just one person. My prayers can't
make a difference"? Many of us think that from time to time.
But it's not true. Esther was the chosen wife of Xerxes, the powerful
king of the Persian Empire. This king had made an example of his
previous wife by banishing her for her disobedience to him. Now
Esther was faced with an even more severe punishment if she dared
approach the king on his throne without being summoned. She was
literally risking her life. Yet her cousin, Mordecai, asked her to do
just that. Her people, the Jews, were in great danger, and Esther was
queen of the empire. "Who knows," her cousin had said, "but that
you have come to royal position for such a time as this?"

Esther was just one person, but she was the one person in the
right place at the right time—put there by God Himself to intercede
for her people. So she called the people together and asked them to
fast and pray for three days. She may have been the queen, but she
still needed great courage, great faith, and God's guidance through
the circumstances. More than her own life was at stake; the lives
of millions of her countrymen were in jeopardy as well. But she
courageously did what she had to do and saved her nation.

As believers, we each have to stand up for what is right, even if the result of our actions may bring ridicule or something worse. It's easy to talk the talk when we're with our Christian friends, but those times when we are surrounded by scoffing unbelievers can be very challenging. Maybe you are the only Christian at work or at a family gathering—what do you do when confronted about your faith? Are you willing to risk banishment by your peers by standing up for what is right?

It would be easier to sit back and quietly wait for the moment to pass—that moment when you could have spoken up for the truth. It's far more challenging to take a risk and stand up for what's right. Esther fasted and prayed and followed God's leading. You can do the same. And you never know when it will result in the very thing for which you were created. You never know when your intercession and actions may save lives.

~~~

Lord, I pray You would help me to be a person who has a heart for You and Your ways, and one who is in the right place at the right time. Enable me, as I fast and pray, to have a powerful effect on the world around me by standing up for what is right and following Your leading. Make my prayers powerful enough to save the lives of the people for whom I pray. Enable me to understand the power of my prayers, and give me the boldness to not hesitate to pray. In Jesus' name I pray.

84

STANDING *in the* GAP
for OUR NATION

*"I looked for a man among them who would build
up the wall and stand before me in the gap on
behalf of the land so I would not have to destroy
it, but I found none" (Ezekiel 22:30).*

It's difficult to read this verse without feeling tremendously sad.
The Lord is speaking through the prophet Ezekiel to the people
of Israel and explaining why judgment could not be averted on their
land. God said He was looking for just one person who would pray
and intercede for the nation so it wouldn't be destroyed, but He
could not find even one person. What a tragedy.

How can we read this passage and not think of our own country
with all its sin and rebellion? Our day of judgment will come as well.
As surely as there is a physical law of gravity, there is also a spiritual
law of reaping what we sow. There may be a time lapse between
what we have sown and what we reap, but the harvest will come.

Bad things don't come from God. They happen because we have
sown bad seeds or as a result of the enemy's work. Either way, God
gives us the opportunity to avert both of those things by standing
in the gap through prayer. In spite of everything that is wrong in
our country, we still enjoy the blessings we have because countless
people have stood in the gap on behalf of our nation.

When God looked for a person to pray and couldn't find *one*, the
land of Israel was taken over by enemies. Do you see how significant a role each of us can play as we learn to pray together for the

protection of our nation today? As we pray according to God's Word and invoke God's power as intercessors, we can affect the outcome of events and avert judgment on our land.

Let's stand in the gap together and see what great things God will do.

⁓

Almighty God, I lift up my nation to You, with all its sin and rebellion, and ask that You will have mercy upon us and help us not reap the full consequences of what we have sown. I stand in the gap to invoke Your power on our behalf. Do not judge us as we deserve, but rather pour out Your Spirit over this land and bring millions of people in humble repentance before You. I know we are deserving of destruction because of how this nation has rejected You and chosen false gods and idols to worship instead, but remember Your people, who have not bent their knees to idols, and hear our prayers of repentance on this nation's behalf. In Jesus' name I pray.

85

WHY WE MUST PRAY
for OUR NATION

∽ Read and Consider ∽
2 Chronicles 7:11-22

*"If my people, who are called by my name, will humble
themselves and pray and seek my face and turn from their
wicked ways, then will I hear from heaven and will forgive
their sin and will heal their land" (2 Chronicles 7:14).*

King Solomon dedicated the temple and saw God's awesome presence there. The people feasted for days and days. The king
prayed a prayer that seemed to cover all possible contingencies,
asking God for guidance, deliverance, and forgiveness. Once the
festivities were over, God answered. Coming to Solomon in the
night, God laid it out, plain and simple. *If* the people would follow
God's ways, *then* He would hear their prayers and heal their land.

Looking back through Israel's history, it is obvious that every
time the people did not follow God's plan, they did not receive
what God had planned for them. When they worshipped other gods
and did whatever they wanted, when they married into other tribes
and made deals with wicked nations, they lost political strength and
were ultimately defeated and taken away as exiles.

We can ask ourselves, how could they have missed it? God couldn't
have been clearer in His instructions. And yet, we too often miss
what God is saying. God is still saying that if we follow His ways
our lives will be better, yet often we don't follow and then wonder
why things go the way they do.

God is still saying, "Pray for your nation." Whether we like our leaders or greatly disagree with them, God calls us to humble ourselves and pray for them.

Our land needs healing. God's promise is that if we turn from our wicked ways, He will forgive and heal. That won't happen without prayer.

Lord God, I come humbly before You and confess the sins of my nation. I pray we as a people would turn from our wicked ways and seek Your face so that You will hear our prayers, forgive our sins, and heal our land. We desperately need Your hand of blessing and protection upon our country. Pour out Your Spirit on us and work Your righteousness in the hearts of the people. Wake up people before it is too late so that we will see that we need to humble ourselves before You in repentance and prayer so that You will avert the judgment on our land that we deserve. In Jesus' name I pray.

86

TEARING DOWN *the* WALL *of* SEPARATION

⁓ Read and Consider ⁓
Isaiah 59:1-8

"But your iniquities have separated you from your God; your sins have hidden his face from you, so that he will not hear" (Isaiah 59:2).

Nothing works in our lives when we don't live God's way, not the least of which is that our prayers are not answered. This verse says that our sins separate us from God so that He will not hear us when we pray. Don't let unconfessed sin separate you from God and hinder your prayers.

If you can't think of any sin in your life, ask God to show you whatever you need to see in that regard. All of us get things in our hearts, souls, minds, attitudes, and emotions that shouldn't be there and are not God's best for our lives. Often we have sin in our hearts and lives and don't even realize it until we start paying the consequences for it. Don't let any separation happen between you and God. Talk to Him daily about the condition of your heart. Ask God often to keep you undeceived. And when He reveals any sin, confess it immediately so that you can be cleansed of it.

We all fail at times, so don't let any failure on your part hinder your prayers in any way. If you take care of this issue by yourself with God in the daytime, by confessing and repenting of all sin as soon as you are aware of it, then you won't have to be dealing with the effects of it when you are trying to sleep at night.

Lord, I know my life does not work when I am not living Your way. Help me to stay undeceived about my own sin so that I can confess it immediately and be cleansed of it. I don't want anything to separate me from You and hinder my prayers by causing You to not hear them. Show me how to tear down any wall of separation that may arise because of sin in my heart. If there is sin in my life I am not recognizing, make it clear to me so that I will not go one more minute causing You to hide Your face from me. In Jesus' name I pray.

87

WHEN *the* FAILURE *of* OTHERS TESTS OUR FAITH

2 Corinthians 13:1-10

"Now we pray to God that you will not do anything wrong. Not that people will see that we have stood the test but that you will do what is right even though we may seem to have failed. For we cannot do anything against the truth, but only for the truth. We are glad whenever we are weak but you are strong; and our prayer is for your perfection" (2 Corinthians 13:7-9).

P aul addressed some criticism that had been spoken against him that had called into question his own faith. This led him to a discussion about passing the test of true faith. He prayed that even if his own faith seemed to fail the test, the faith of the Corinthians would not waver but instead remain strong.

Paul's prayer encouraging the Corinthians to do what was right was not the prayer of a perfectionistic leader who felt that the behavior of those he trained reflected on him. His prayer had to do with urging them on to authentic faith and not being dependent on him. Too often we become so connected to the people who mentor or teach us spiritually that when they fail in our eyes, our faith may fail too. But Paul's prayer was that the faith of these people would be so connected to *God* and to *His* faithfulness that nothing, not even disappointments in their mentors, could shake it.

We all need that kind of faith. People will let us down from time to time—even the best mentors, even our favorite preachers, even the people we need the most will disappoint us. But that won't shake us if the foundation of our faith is in God alone.

To have that kind of faith, we must invest in our relationship with Him. He will never change. We can always depend on Him. He won't fail us. If we ask Him to, He will strengthen *our* faith so we can lift up others who are struggling with *theirs*.

∂∞⊃C∞∿

Lord God, when I see the failure of any servant of Yours, I pray it will not shake my faith in the least. Help me to do the right thing and remain strong in You no matter what I see anyone else doing. Give me faith that is not dependent on the rise or fall of others. I know You won't fail, even though others do, and that is all that matters. Thank You that You never change and I can depend on You. Thank You that You will not fail, even though I see other sons and daughters of Yours who do. Help me to be strong in my faith to help others who are weak in theirs. In Jesus' name I pray.

88

BOASTING *in* GOD ALONE

Jeremiah 9:13-26

*"This is what the LORD says: 'Let not the wise man boast of
his wisdom or the strong man boast of his strength or the
rich man boast of his riches, but let him who boasts boast
about this: that he understands and knows me, that I am
the LORD, who exercises kindness, justice and righteousness
on earth, for in these I delight'" (Jeremiah 9:23-24).*

Everyone wants to accomplish something significant with his life.
We all desire to do things well. Who doesn't want to accomplish
something worth boasting about, even if we are not the ones doing
the boasting? But God says we are to boast about one thing only,
and this is that we know *Him.*

Men and women of the world boast about their accomplishments.
These verses mention three things people commonly boast about,
and those are wisdom, strength, and riches. But even if we have *all*
of these characteristics, we can't get prideful about them as though
we did something great. That's because everything we have comes
from God.

The one thing we can brag about is that we have a relationship
with the Lord. The only reason we have the potential to do something great is that we are His and His Spirit dwells in us. Because
of His greatness *in* us, He will accomplish great things *through* us.
Perhaps the greatest things we will do in life are acts that no one
will ever know about—such as interceding in prayer or caring for
the needy—the impact of which we will not comprehend this side
of eternity.

*God, I confess any pride I have in my life, for I know
all the good things I have come from You. Help me to
never even appear to boast about anything other than
the fact that I know You. And the only reason I have
the potential to do something good is because Your
Holy Spirit dwells in me. Your Word is clear about
how much You hate pride, and I do not want to ever
fall into that. I know it is only Your greatness in me
that causes great things to happen through me.
In Jesus' name I pray.*

89

PRAYING *in the* GOOD TIMES

∾ Read and Consider ∾

2 Chronicles 15

*"Although he did not remove the high places
from Israel, Asa's heart was fully committed to
the LORD all his life" (2 Chronicles 15:17).*

When we live a lifestyle of praise and worship, we keep our heart fresh and open to the working of the Holy Spirit in us. Spending time in prayerful worship keeps us in the right attitude to hear from God and be guided by Him. It positions Him as first priority in our lives and helps us stay dependent upon Him, whether things in our lives are going well or not.

When the Spirit of God came upon the prophet Azariah, he told King Asa, "The LORD is with you when you are with him. If you seek him, he will be found by you, but if you forsake him, he will forsake you" (15:2). It can't get any clearer than that. If God is with *us* as long as we're with *Him,* that should increase our motivation to be with *Him.*

So what does it mean to be "with God"? We understand it pretty clearly in the bad times. We come to God desperate for help. What about when things are going well? The best advice when you are in a season of peace and rest is to use that time to build and fortify yourself in the Lord. Study His Word. Communicate with Him in prayer. Spend time in His presence in worship and praise. Get closer. Stay *with* Him. Use that time to fall in love with Jesus all over again.

King Asa didn't always do everything right, but in the end he was described as a king who had a heart fully committed to the Lord.

Even when you don't act perfectly, you can show God that your heart is perfectly in love with Him by the praise you give Him every day.

Father God, I worship You and thank You that You are the God of love. Your love in my life has saved me and is transforming me for Your high purpose. Help me to remember to pray as fervently to You in the good times as I do in the difficult times. Teach me to always keep my heart open to what You are doing in my life. Enable me to be fully committed to You at all times so there is no place in my heart for anything that wants to exalt itself above You. In Jesus' name I pray.

90

PRAYING *for* PEOPLE WHO NEED GOOD NEWS

Read and Consider
---
2 Thessalonians 3:1-5

*"Finally, brothers, pray for us that the message of
the Lord may spread rapidly and be honored, just
as it was with you" (2 Thessalonians 3:1).*

Do you remember the first time you heard about Jesus and His
message of salvation, when the Good News really penetrated
your soul? Do you recall that pivotal moment when your life changed
for all eternity? Who brought Jesus' message to you? How did God
use that person to reach out and touch your heart?

God is always intensely personal and masterfully creative in the
ways He reaches out to us. Each one of us has a unique and wonderful story of our salvation. And all of our stories have one thing in
common: Somewhere, somehow, *someone* responded to God's call to
spread His love and bring His message. Whether we heard a pastor
who preached a message that affected us or listened to a friend who
talked to us about Jesus or someone gave us a Bible or a Christian
book or a person was praying for us...someone reached out because
of a desire to help us discover the truth about God's love.

In this passage, the apostle Paul asked fellow Christians to pray
for those who were spreading the message of the Lord, that it would
be far-reaching and effective, "just as it was with you." This is a
strong reminder to remember how Jesus saved us and all that He
has done for us so that we will deeply desire that others experience
His love too.

Praying is the most important thing you can do when trying to reach people for the Lord. Whether you feel confident or not about your own efforts to spread the good news, your prayers will pave the way for hearts to open up and receive what God wants to speak to them. Whether you are in the front lines of evangelism or behind the scenes, as long as you are praying, you are a vital part of God's work here on earth. Along with everything else you are doing for the Lord, don't forget to share your own story about how you came to know Jesus. Tell it often. And let it remind you to pray for those who are searching for truth and need to hear about all the good news Jesus has for them.

Lord, use me to bring the good news of salvation through Your Son, Jesus Christ, to others. Just as You have used others powerfully in my life, equip me with the right words at the right time so that those whose hearts are ready will be drawn toward You. I also pray for the men and women who need the good news, that their hearts would be open to receive all You have for them. Show me anyone in my life who needs that lifeline extended to them so that I can help them, whether through prayer or with my own personal words to them.
In Jesus' name I pray.

91

The IMPORTANCE *of*
SPIRITUAL AUTHORITY

Read and Consider
1 Corinthians 11:2-10

*"For this reason, and because of the angels, the
woman ought to have a sign of authority
on her head" (1 Corinthians 11:10).*

Paul wrote that women should have a sign of authority on their
heads. This refers to spiritual authority, and it is still very important today. While we may not actually put a covering over our heads,
we must submit to divinely appointed authority. It's part of God's
order. God won't pour into our lives all He has for us until we are
in a right relationship with the proper authority figures He has
placed in our lives. They are there for our protection and benefit.
God's power is too precious and too powerful to be let loose in an
unsubmitted soul.

Women need this spiritual covering. It protects them from the
enemy of their soul. When spiritual covering is done right—with
strength, humility, kindness, and respect, and not with abuse, arrogance, harshness, or lovelessness—it becomes a place of safety for a
woman. It brings a right order to her life.

More and more believing women are being given an open door to
become all they were created to be. They are moving out in different
areas of expertise and ministry and making important differences
in their realms of influence. They are realizing that they are not just
an afterthought in the order of God's creation, but were created for
a special purpose. More and more they are enabled to fulfill their
destiny because more men are rising up to their place of spiritual

authority and leadership. This is an answer to the prayers of countless women and something for which everyone must praise God. If a woman will trust God's power to flow through the authorities He has placed over her, she can bloom and grow and change her world by the power of God's Spirit. Pray to be in right order with the spiritual authority in your life.

∿∿

Lord, help me to be in right relationship to the authority figures You have put in my life. I know they are there for my protection. I want my life to be in perfect order so I am submitted in the right way. I don't want to do anything that would delay or prevent my becoming all You created me to be. We all need a spiritual covering, whether through a pastor or spiritually mature leader in Your kingdom. Help me to always be in right relationship to You and to those You have put in my life. In Jesus' name I pray.

92

LEARNING *to* PRAY BOLDLY

∽ Read and Consider ∼
1 Kings 17

*"Now Elijah the Tishbite, from Tishbe in Gilead, said
to Ahab, 'As the LORD, the God of Israel, lives, whom
I serve, there will be neither dew nor rain in the next
few years except at my word'" (1 Kings 17:1).*

When Elijah prayed, things happened. Clouds dried up or gushed rain, ravens served as food waiters, oil and flour multiplied, fire fell from heaven, and a dead boy came back to life. Some of these miracles were examples of divine timing, and each one of them was an example of divine power. All of them remind us that nothing is impossible when God decides to act.

When people and churches make prayer a priority, they always see answers to their prayers. Those who pray boldly may have the thrill of seeing miracles. When people are unified in the spirit of praise and they pray in unity, God does amazing things. Some people may question that God would really change the weather because people prayed. But He did it in the Bible. "Elijah was a man just like us. He prayed earnestly that it would not rain, and it did not rain on the land for three and a half years. Again he prayed, and the heavens gave rain, and the earth produced its crops" (James 5:17-18). If Elijah was like us, then why can't we pray like he prayed? We don't have to understand everything about how prayer works; we just have to believe that it does. Most of us know little about car engines, but that doesn't keep us from driving. We just have to turn the key. Few of us understand electricity, but we still expect our appliances to work when we plug them in. Prayer is the key that gets things going. Prayer is the way we plug in to the power of God. We are instructed to "pray continually" (1 Thessalonians 5:17). And God has promised to hear and answer. Elijah saw some unique answers to prayer, but his ability to pray was not unique. When you pray, big things can happen too. That's because God hears and will answer according to His will.

Lord, I know You are the God of miracles and nothing is impossible for those who pray in the power of Your Spirit. Help me to pray boldly and believe for miracles in answer to my prayers. Teach me how to not pray too small. I don't want my prayers to stop short of what You want to see happen in my life and in the lives of those for whom I pray. I want to be a person who prays and things happen. Help me keep my life pure and in right order so that nothing interferes with how You want to use me for Your purposes. In Jesus' name I pray.

93

THANK GOD *for* HIS LOVE

Zephaniah 3:8-20

*"The LORD your God is with you, he is mighty to save. He
will take great delight in you, he will quiet you with his love,
he will rejoice over you with singing" (Zephaniah 3:17).*

The Lord is with you. What joy there is in knowing that God is
with you! You always have a line of open communication with
Him because He is omnipresent. Whether your prayers are long or
short, the Lord hears them all. Thank Him that He is a God who
is close to you.

The Lord is mighty to save. Rejoice that you have been snatched
from the jaws of hell because of God's great love. He has provided
salvation through His Son, Jesus Christ, and He accepts your repentance for sin no matter how many times you come to Him with
a repentant heart. Thank Him for His salvation and continuing
forgiveness.

*The Lord takes great delight in you...He will rejoice over you with
singing.* Just as you rejoice in the victories of others, God will rejoice
over you with gladness. Like the Father that He is, He is proud of
His children. He is glad when you follow His will and live a life
that will cause others to want to know Him. Thank Him for His
joyful delight in you.

The Lord will quiet you with His love. In times of turmoil, if you
turn to the Lord, He will quiet you with His love. There is peace in
knowing that whatever circumstances come your way, God will be
there to guide you through. In good times and bad, His love will

comfort your pain and soothe your weariness. Thank Him for His peace in you.

Rejoice daily in this profound relationship you have with the Almighty God. Thank Him again and again for His presence and love in your life, even when you know you don't deserve it.

Lord, I have great joy in knowing You are always with me and have the power to save me from the plans of the enemy. Help me to remember at all times—even when I go through difficult situations that shake the very foundation of my soul—that my foundation is in You and my security is sustained by Your great love for me. Thank You that in tough times Your love will give me peace, and Your Spirit will guide me through them. In Jesus' name I pray.

94

BEING REMEMBERED *in* PRAYER

ᴄ∾ Read and Consider ∿ᴄ
---
2 Timothy 1:3-7

"I thank God, whom I serve, as my forefathers did,
with a clear conscience, as night and day I constantly
remember you in my prayers" (2 Timothy 1:3).

We all want to be remembered. We all desire to make a positive and lasting impression on someone's life. None of us wants to be forgotten by the people who are near and dear to us—especially family and friends. And who doesn't want to make a profound impact on the world in some way? But most importantly, we all want to be remembered by others in prayer.

Imagine being remembered day and night in prayer. Think of how loved and cared for you would feel. When we are prayed for, we *feel* those prayers—even if we don't know people are praying, even if we don't fully understand what it is we are feeling. When we lift up each other in prayer, we are not only bound *together* in the love of God, but we also deepen and strengthen our *personal* bond with the Lord. We form a prayer circle with God at the center, and it grows stronger every time we pray. We experience great blessings whether we are the giver or the receiver of prayer.

If you need to be reminded to pray for others, keep a prayer journal with a list of the people who need your prayers and how you want to pray for them. Then pray as the Spirit leads. It's inspiring to think how Paul constantly remembered to pray for Timothy. We can do the same with people in our own lives.

Lord, help me to not forget anyone in my prayers. Especially show me the people who feel forgotten so that I can lift them before You in intercession. Bring specific people to mind who need a miracle of healing or help. Show me who needs to hear Your voice guiding them. Enable the people I pray for to sense Your love in their lives. Thank You that as I lift up other people You bring to my mind, that brings blessings to my own life as well. In Jesus' name I pray.

95

A PARTING PRAYER

∽ Read and Consider ∼
Acts 21:1-16

*"But when our time was up, we left and continued
on our way. All the disciples and their wives and
children accompanied us out of the city, and there
on the beach we knelt to pray" (Acts 21:5).*

Paul and some believers in Tyre had a chance to meet up as Paul
was passing through and have fellowship for a week. The Holy
Spirit allowed these Christians to foresee the persecution Paul would
endure in Jerusalem (his destination), and they urged him not to go
there. They were worried about his safety and wanted to keep him
from harm. But Paul knew where the Lord wanted him to go, and
he would not be swayed from his purpose. As he departed, all of
the disciples and their families accompanied him to the ship, where
they knelt on the beach to pray before saying goodbye.

What better way to part from someone than to kneel in prayer?
These friends knew the dangers that lay ahead for Paul—and perhaps
eventually for them as persecution clouds began to build. Perhaps
they prayed for safety, but they surely also prayed for guidance and
boldness as they continued to work for the Lord, spreading His
message throughout the land. Perhaps they prayed that God would
bring them back together in fellowship again. And we know that
they prayed for each other when they were apart—Paul says so in
his letters.

We should remember to pray for people whenever we part from
them or they part from us. We can pray for our spouse as he or she
heads off to work. We can pray for our children as they go to school.

We can pray for our friends as they go about their daily business. We can pray for our guests as they leave our home. Prayer is the most powerful tool we have as believers—our direct link with God. Let's not neglect it as we part from others.

⁓⁓⁓⚬⚬⚬⁓⁓⁓

*Dear God, help me to remember when I am with people
who are about to leave on a journey—no matter how
long or short—that I need to pray for them to have
safety and guidance. Help me to not forget to pray for
my own family members who are leaving the home
to start their day, or any guests in my house who are
leaving to get about their business or travel home. Teach
me never to hesitate to pray for others because we
never know what the day may bring or what plans the
enemy is trying to erect around us all. But You do.
In Jesus' name I pray.*

Prayer Journal

While you are reading through the devotions in this book, you may want to write down what God speaks to your heart, or some insights or thoughts you would like to remember. And as you pray the prayers in this book, you will surely think of other things you want to pray about and people you need to pray for, and you can write it all down here. The following pages are for your convenience.

_____

_____

_____

_____

_____

_____

_____

_____

_____

Other Books by Stormie Omartian

OUT OF DARKNESS

Anyone who has been scarred by the past or feels imprisoned by deep emotional needs will find hope and help in this personal journey. It is a glorious story of how God can bring life out of death, light out of darkness.

LEAD ME, HOLY SPIRIT

Stormie has written books on prayer that have helped millions of people talk to God. Now she focuses on the Holy Spirit and how He wants you to listen to His gentle leading when He speaks to your heart, soul, and spirit. He wants to help you enter into the relationship with God you yearn for and the wholeness and freedom He has for you. He wants to lead you into a better life than you could ever possibly live without Him.

PRAYER WARRIOR

Stormie says, "There is already a war going on around you, and you are in it whether you want to be or not. There is a spiritual war of good and evil—between God and His enemy—and God wants us to stand strong on His side, the side that wins. We win the war when we pray in power because prayer *is* the battle." This book will help you become a powerful prayer warrior who understands the path to victory.

THE PRAYING WOMAN'S DEVOTIONAL

This collection of devotions will give you short reflections on Bible passages that will remind you of all the magnificent and miraculous things God has done. And it will help you see what God not only can do in *your* life, but what He can do in the world around you in response to your faith-filled prayers.

To learn more about Harvest House books and
to read sample chapters, visit our website:

www.harvesthousepublishers.com

HARVEST HOUSE PUBLISHERS
EUGENE, OREGON